THREE PLAYS

BY

SEAN O'CASEY

JUNO AND THE PAYCOCK
THE SHADOW OF A GUNMAN
THE PLOUGH AND THE STARS

M

PAPERMAC

Juno and the Paycock and *The Shadow of a Gunman*
first published 1925
The Plough and the Stars first published 1926

This collection first published 1957 by St Martin's Library

First published in Pocket Papermacs 1966 by Macmillan London Ltd

This edition published 1994 by Papermac
a division of Pan Macmillan Publishers Limited
Cavaye Place London SW10 9PG
and Basingstoke

Associated companies throughout the world

ISBN 0–330–61616–2

3 5 7 9 8 6 4

A CIP catalogue record for this book is available from
the British Library

Printed and bound in Great Britain by
Cox & Wyman Ltd, Reading, Berkshire

CONTENTS

JUNO AND THE PAYCOCK

A Tragedy in Three Acts

CHARACTERS IN THE PLAY

'Captain' Jack Boyle
Juno Boyle, *his wife*
Johnny Boyle } *their children*
Mary Boyle
'Joxer' Daly
Mrs. Maisie Madigan
'Needle' Nugent, *a tailor*
Mrs. Tancred
} *Residents in the Tenement*

Jerry Devine
Charles Bentham, *a school teacher*
An Irregular Mobilizer
Two Irregulars
A Coal-block Vendor
A Sewing Machine Man
Two Furniture Removal Men
Two Neighbours

SCENE

Act I.—The living apartment of a two-roomed tenancy of the Boyle family, in a tenement house in Dublin.

Act II.—The same.

Act III.—The same.

A few days elapse between Acts I and II, and two months between Acts II and III.

During Act III the curtain is lowered for a few minutes to denote the lapse of one hour.

Period of the play, 1922.

ACT I

The living-room of a two-room tenancy occupied by the Boyle family in a tenement house in Dublin. Left, a door leading to another part of the house; left of door a window looking into the street; at back a dresser; farther to right at back, a window looking into the back of the house. Between the window and the dresser is a picture of the Virgin; below the picture, on a bracket, is a crimson bowl in which a floating votive light is burning. Farther to the right is a small bed partly concealed by cretonne hangings strung on a twine. To the right is the fireplace; near the fireplace is a door leading to the other room. Beside the fireplace is a box containing coal. On the mantelshelf is an alarm clock lying on its face. In a corner near the window looking into the back is a galvanized bath. A table and some chairs. On the table are breakfast things for one. A teapot is on the hob and a frying-pan stands inside the fender. There are a few books on the dresser and one on the table. Leaning against the dresser is a long-handled shovel—the kind invariably used by labourers when turning concrete or mixing mortar. Johnny Boyle is sitting crouched beside the fire. Mary with her jumper off—it is lying on the back of a chair—is arranging her hair before a tiny mirror perched on the table. Beside the mirror is stretched out the morning paper, which she looks at when she isn't gazing into the mirror. She is a well-made and good-looking girl of twenty-two. Two forces are working in her mind—one, through the circumstances of her life, pulling her back; the other, through the influence of books she has read, pushing her forward. The opposing forces are apparent in her speech and her manners, both of which are degraded by her environment, and improved by her acquaintance—slight though it be—with literature. The time is early forenoon.

Mary (*looking at the paper*). On a little by-road, out beyant Finglas, he was found.

> [*Mrs. Boyle enters by door on right; she has been shopping and carries a small parcel in her hand. She is forty-five years of age, and twenty years ago she must have been a pretty woman; but her face has now assumed that look which ultimately settles down upon the faces of the women of the working-class; a look of listless monotony and harassed anxiety, blending with an expression of mechanical resistance. Were circumstances favourable, she would probably be a handsome, active and clever woman.*]

Mrs. Boyle. Isn't he come in yet?

Mary. No, mother.

Mrs. Boyle. Oh, he'll come in when he likes; struttin' about the town like a paycock with Joxer, I suppose. I hear all about Mrs. Tancred's son is in this mornin's paper.

Mary. The full details are in it this mornin'; seven wounds he had—one entherin' the neck, with an exit wound beneath the left shoulder-blade; another in the left breast penethratin' the heart, an' . . .

Johnny (*springing up from the fire*). Oh, quit that readin' for God's sake! Are yous losin' all your feelin's? It'll soon be that none of you'll read anythin' that's not about butcherin'!

> [*He goes quickly into the room on left.*

Mary. He's gettin' very sensitive, all of a sudden!

Mrs. Boyle. I'll read it myself, Mary, by an' by, when I come home. Everybody's sayin' that he was a Diehard—thanks be to God that Johnny had nothin' to do with him this long time. . . . (*Opening the parcel and taking out some sausages, which she places on a plate*) Ah, then, if that father o' yours doesn't come in soon for his breakfast, he may go without any; I'll not wait much longer for him.

Mary. Can't you let him get it himself when he comes in?

Mrs. Boyle. Yes, an' let him bring in Joxer Daly along with him? Ay, that's what he'd like an' that's what he's

waitin' for—till he thinks I'm gone to work, an' then sail in
with the boul' Joxer, to burn all the coal an' dhrink all the
tea in the place, to show them what a good Samaritan he is!
But I'll stop here till he comes in, if I have to wait till to-
morrow mornin'.

Voice of Johnny inside.   Mother!

Mrs. Boyle.   Yis?

Voice of Johnny.   Bring us in a dhrink o' wather.

Mrs. Boyle.   Bring in that fella a dhrink o' wather, for God's
sake, Mary.

Mary.   Isn't he big an' able enough to come out an' get it
himself?

Mrs. Boyle.   If you weren't well yourself you'd like somebody to bring you in a dhrink o' wather.

[*She brings in drink and returns.*

Mrs. Boyle.   Isn't it terrible to have to be waitin' this way!
You'd think he was bringin' twenty poun's a week into the
house the way he's going on.   He wore out the Health Insurance long ago, he's afther wearin' out the unemployment
dole, an', now, he's thryin' to wear out me!   An' constantly singin', no less, when he ought always to be on his
knees offerin' up a Novena for a job!

Mary (*trying a ribbon fillet-wise around her head*).   I don't like
this ribbon, ma; I think I'll wear the green—it looks betther
than the blue.

Mrs. Boyle.   Ah, wear whatever ribbon you like, girl, only
don't be botherin' me.   I don't know what a girl on strike
wants to be wearin' a ribbon round her head for, or silk
stockin's on her legs either; it's wearin' them things that make
the employers think they're givin' yous too much money.

Mary.   The hour is past now when we'll ask the employers'
permission to wear what we like.

Mrs. Boyle.   I don't know why you wanted to walk out for
Jennie Claffey; up to this you never had a good word for her.

Mary.   What's the use of belongin' to a Trades Union if

you won't stand up for your principles? Why did they sack her? It was a clear case of victimization. We couldn't let her walk the streets, could we?

Mrs. Boyle. No, of course yous couldn't—yous wanted to keep her company. Wan victim wasn't enough. When the employers sacrifice wan victim, the Trades Unions go wan betther be sacrificin' a hundred.

Mary. It doesn't matther what you say, ma—a principle's a principle.

Mrs. Boyle. Yis; an' when I go into oul' Murphy's to-morrow, an' he gets to know that, instead o' payin' all, I'm goin' to borry more, what'll he say when I tell him a principle's a principle? What'll we do if he refuses to give us any more on tick?

Mary. He daren't refuse—if he does, can't you tell him he's paid?

Mrs. Boyle. It's lookin' as if he was paid, whether he refuses or no.

[Johnny *appears at the door on left. He can be plainly seen now; he is a thin, delicate fellow, something younger than* Mary. *He has evidently gone through a rough time. His face is pale and drawn; there is a tremulous look of indefinite fear in his eyes. The left sleeve of his coat is empty, and he walks with a slight halt.*

Johnny. I was lyin' down; I thought yous were gone. Oul' Simon Mackay is thrampin' about like a horse over me head, an' I can't sleep with him—they're like thunder-claps in me brain! The curse o'—God forgive me for goin' to curse!

Mrs. Boyle. There, now; go back an' lie down again an' I'll bring you in a nice cup o' tay.

Johnny. Tay, tay, tay! You're always thinkin' o' tay. If a man was dyin', you'd thry to make him swally a cup o' tay! [He goes back.

Mrs. Boyle. I don't know what's goin' to be done with him. The bullet he got in the hip in Easter Week was bad enough;

but the bomb that shatthered his arm in the fight in O'Connell Street put the finishin' touch on him. . I knew he was makin' a fool of himself. God knows I went down on me bended knees to him not to go agen the Free State.

Mary. He stuck to his principles, an', no matther how you may argue, ma, a principle's a principle.

Voice of Johnny. Is Mary goin' to stay here?

Mary. No, I'm not goin' to stay here; you can't expect me to be always at your beck an' call, can you?

Voice of Johnny. I won't stop here be meself!

Mrs. Boyle. Amn't I nicely handicapped with the whole o' yous! I don't know what any o' yous ud do without your ma. (*To* Johnny) Your father'll be here in a minute, an' if you want anythin',' he'll get it for you.

Johnny. I hate assin' him for anythin' . . . He hates to be assed to stir. . . . Is the light lightin' before the picture o' the Virgin?

Mrs. Boyle. Yis, yis! The wan inside to St. Anthony isn't enough, but he must have another wan to the Virgin here!

> [Jerry Devine *enters hastily. He is about twenty-five, well set, active and earnest. He is a type, becoming very common now in the Labour Movement, of a mind knowing enough to make the mass of his associates, who know less, a power, and too little to broaden that power for the benefit of all.* Mary *seizes her jumper and runs hastily into room left.*

Jerry (*breathless*). Where's the Captain, Mrs. Boyle, where's the Captain?

Mrs. Boyle. You may well ass a body that: he's wherever Joxer Daly is—dhrinkin' in some snug or another.

Jerry. Father Farrell is just afther stoppin' to tell me to run up an' get him to go to the new job that's goin' on in Rathmines; his cousin is foreman o' the job, an' Father Farrell was speakin' to him about poor Johnny an' his father bein' idle so long, an' the foreman told Father Farrell to send

the Captain up an' he'd give him a start—I wondher where I'd
find him?

Mrs. Boyle. You'll find he's ayther in Ryan's or Foley's.

Jerry. I'll run round to Ryan's—I know it's a great
house o' Joxer's.   [*He rushes out.*

Mrs. Boyle (*piteously*). There now, he'll miss that job, or
I know for what! If he gets win' o' the word, he'll not
come back till evenin', so that it'll be too late. There'll
never be any good got out o' him so long as he goes with that
shouldher-shruggin' Joxer. I killin' meself workin', an' he
sthruttin' about from mornin' till night like a paycock!

> [*The steps of two persons are heard coming up a flight of
> stairs. They are the footsteps of* Captain Boyle *and*
> Joxer. Captain Boyle *is singing in a deep, sonorous,
> self-honouring voice.*

The Captain. Sweet Spirit, hear me prayer! Hear . . .
oh . . . hear . . . me prayer . . . hear, oh, hear . . . Oh,
he . . . ar . . . oh, he . . . ar . . . me . . . pray . . . er!

Joxer (*outside*). Ah, that's a darlin' song, a daaarlin' song!

Mrs. Boyle (*viciously*). Sweet spirit hear his prayer! Ah,
then, I'll take me solemn affeydavey, it's not for a job he's
prayin'!

> [*She sits down on the bed so that the cretonne hangings hide
> her from the view of those entering.*

> [*The* Captain *comes in. He is a man of about sixty;
> stout, grey-haired and stocky. His neck is short, and his
> head looks like a stone ball that one sometimes sees on top
> of a gate-post. His cheeks, reddish-purple, are puffed out,
> as if he were always repressing an almost irrepressible
> ejaculation. On his upper lip is a crisp, tightly cropped
> moustache; he carries himself with the upper part of his body
> slightly thrown back, and his stomach slightly thrust for-
> ward. His walk is a slow, consequential strut. His
> clothes are dingy, and he wears a faded seaman's-cap with a
> glazed peak.*

Boyle (to Joxer, who is still outside). Come on, come on in, Joxer; she's gone out long ago, man. If there's nothing else to be got, we'll furrage out a cup o' tay, anyway. It's the only bit I get in comfort when she's away. 'Tisn't Juno should be her pet name at all, but Deirdre of the Sorras, for she's always grousin'.

> [Joxer *steps cautiously into the room. He may be younger than the* Captain *but he looks a lot older. His face is like a bundle of crinkled paper; his eyes have a cunning twinkle; he is spare and loosely built; he has a habit of constantly shrugging his shoulders with a peculiar twitching movement, meant to be ingratiating. His face is invariably ornamented with a grin.*

Joxer. It's a terrible thing to be tied to a woman that's always grousin'. I don't know how you stick it—it ud put years on me. It's a good job she has to be so ofen away, for *(with a shrug)* when the cat's away, the mice can play!

Boyle (with a commanding and complacent gesture). Pull over to the fire, Joxer, an' we'll have a cup o' tay in a minute.

Joxer. Ah, a cup o' tay's a darlin' thing, a daaarlin' thing —the cup that cheers but doesn't . . .

> [Joxer's *rhapsody is cut short by the sight of* Juno *coming forward and confronting the two cronies. Both are stupefied.*

Mrs. Boyle (with sweet irony—poking the fire, and turning her head to glare at Joxer). Pull over to the fire, Joxer Daly, an' we'll have a cup o' tay in a minute! Are you sure, now, you wouldn't like an egg?

Joxer. I can't stop, Mrs. Boyle; I'm in a desperate hurry, a desperate hurry.

Mrs. Boyle. Pull over to the fire, Joxer Daly; people is always far more comfortabler here than they are in their own place.

> [Joxer *makes hastily for the door.* Boyle *stirs to follow him; thinks of something to relieve the situation—stops, and says suddenly:*

Joxer!

Joxer (at door ready to bolt). Yis?

Boyle. You know the foreman o' that job that's goin' on down in Killesther, don't you, Joxer?

Joxer (puzzled). Foreman—Killesther?

Boyle (with a meaning look). He's a butty o' yours, isn't he?

Joxer (the truth dawning on him). The foreman at Killesther —oh yis, yis. He's an oul' butty o' mine—oh, he's a darlin' man, a daarlin' man.

Boyle. Oh, then, it's a sure thing. It's a pity we didn't go down at breakfast first thing this mornin'—we might ha' been working now; but you didn't know it then.

Joxer (with a shrug). It's betther late than never.

Boyle. It's nearly time we got a start, anyhow; I'm fed up knockin' round, doin' nothin'. He promised you—gave you the straight tip?

Joxer. Yis. 'Come down on the blow o' dinner,' says he, 'an' I'll start you, an' any friend you like to brin' with you.' 'Ah,' says I, 'you're a darlin' man, a daaarlin' man.'

Boyle. Well, it couldn't come at a betther time—we're a long time waitin' for it.

Joxer. Indeed we were; but it's a long lane that has no turnin'.

Boyle. The blow up for dinner is at one—wait till I see what time it 'tis.

    [He goes over to the mantelpiece, and gingerly lifts the clock.

Mrs. Boyle. Min' now, how you go on fiddlin' with that clock—you know the least little thing sets it asthray.

Boyle. The job couldn't come at a betther time; I'm feelin' in great fettle, Joxer. I'd hardly believe I ever had a pain in me legs, an' last week I was nearly crippled with them.

Joxer. That's betther an' betther; ah, God never shut wan door but He opened another!

Boyle. It's only eleven o'clock; we've lashin's o' time. I'll slip on me oul' moleskins afther breakfast, an' we can saunther down at our ayse. (*Putting his hand on the shovel*) I think, Joxer, we'd betther bring our shovels?

Joxer. Yis, Captain, yis; it's betther to go fully prepared an' ready for all eventualities. You bring your long-tailed shovel, an' I'll bring me navvy. We mighten' want them, an', then agen, we might: for want of a nail the shoe was lost, for want of a shoe the horse was lost, an' for want of a horse the man was lost—aw, that's a darlin' proverb, a daarlin' . . .

[*As* Joxer *is finishing his sentence,* Mrs. Boyle *approaches the door and* Joxer *retreats hurriedly. She shuts the door with a bang.*

Boyle (*suggestively*). We won't be long pullin' ourselves together agen when I'm working for a few weeks.

[Mrs. Boyle *takes no notice.*

Boyle. The foreman on the job is an oul' butty o' Joxer's; I have an idea that I know him meself. (*Silence*) . . . There's a button off the back o' me moleskin trousers. . . . If you leave out a needle an' thread I'll sew it on meself. . . . Thanks be to God, the pains in me legs is gone, anyhow!

Mrs. Boyle (*with a burst*). Look here, Mr. Jacky Boyle, them yarns won't go down with Juno. I know you an' Joxer Daly of an oul' date, an' if you think you're able to come it over me with them fairy tales, you're in the wrong shop.

Boyle (*coughing subduedly to relieve the tenseness of the situation*). U-u-u-ugh!

Mrs. Boyle. Butty o' Joxer's! Oh, you'll do a lot o' good as long as you continue to be a butty o' Joxer's!

Boyle. U-u-u-ugh!

Mrs. Boyle. Shovel! Ah, then, me boyo, you'd do far more work with a knife an' fork than ever you'll do with a shovel! If there was e'er a genuine job goin' you'd be dh'other way about—not able to lift your arms with the pains in your legs! Your poor wife slavin' to keep the bit in your mouth, an' you gallivantin' about all the day like a paycock!

Boyle. It ud be betther for a man to be dead, betther for a man to be dead.

Mrs. Boyle (ignoring the interruption). Everybody callin' you 'Captain', an' you only wanst on the wather, in an oul' collier from here to Liverpool, when anybody, to listen or look at you, ud take you for a second Christo For Columbus!

Boyle. Are you never goin' to give us a rest?

Mrs. Boyle. Oh, you're never tired o' lookin' for a rest.

Boyle. D'ye want to dhrive me out o' the house?

Mrs. Boyle. It ud be easier to dhrive you out o' the house than to dhrive you into a job. Here, sit down an' take your breakfast—it may be the last you'll get, for I don't know where the next is goin' to come from.

Boyle. If I get this job we'll be all right.

Mrs. Boyle. Did ye see Jerry Devine?

Boyle (testily). No, I didn't see him.

Mrs. Boyle. No, but you seen Joxer. Well, he was here lookin' for you.

Boyle. Well, let him look!

Mrs. Boyle. Oh, indeed, he may well look, for it ud be hard for him to see you, an' you stuck in Ryan's snug.

Boyle. I wasn't in Ryan's snug—I don't go into Ryan's.

Mrs. Boyle. Oh, is there a mad dog there? Well, if you weren't in Ryan's you were in Foley's.

Boyle. I'm telling you for the last three weeks I haven't tasted a dhrop of intoxicatin' liquor. I wasn't in ayther wan snug or dh'other—I could swear that on a prayer-book—I'm as innocent as the child unborn!

Mrs. Boyle. Well, if you'd been in for your breakfast you'd ha' seen him.

Boyle (suspiciously). What does he want me for?

Mrs. Boyle. He'll be back any minute an' then you'll soon know.

Boyle. I'll dhrop out an' see if I can meet him.

Mrs. Boyle. You'll sit down an' take your breakfast, an'
let me go to me work, for I'm an hour late already waitin' for
you.

Boyle. You needn't ha' waited, for I'll take no breakfast
—I've a little spirit left in me still!

Mrs. Boyle. Are you goin' to have your breakfast—yes or
no?

Boyle (*too proud to yield*). I'll have no breakfast—yous can
keep your breakfast. (*Plaintively*) I'll knock out a bit somewhere, never fear.

Mrs. Boyle. Nobody's goin' to coax you—don't think that.
          [*She vigorously replaces the pan and the sausages in the press.*

Boyle. I've a little spirit left in me still.

                              [Jerry Devine *enters hastily.*

Jerry. Oh, here you are at last! I've been searchin' for
you everywhere. The foreman in Foley's told me you
hadn't left the snug with Joxer ten minutes before I went in.

Mrs. Boyle. An' he swearin' on the holy prayer-book that
he wasn't in no snug!

Boyle (*to* Jerry). What business is it o' yours whether I was
in a snug or no? What do you want to be gallopin' about
afther me for? Is a man not to be allowed to leave his house
for a minute without havin' a pack o' spies, pimps an' in-
formers cantherin' at his heels?

Jerry. Oh, you're takin' a wrong view of it, Mr. Boyle;
I simply was anxious to do you a good turn. I have a
message for you from Father Farrell: He says that if you go to
the job that's on in Rathmines, an' ask for Foreman Managan,
you'll get a start.

Boyle. That's all right, but I don't want the motions of
me body to be watched the way an asthronomer ud watch a
star. If you're folleyin' Mary aself, you've no pereeogative
to be folleyin' me. (*Suddenly catching his thigh*) U-ugh, I'm
afther gettin' a terrible twinge in me right leg!

Mrs. Boyle. Oh, it won't be very long now till it travels into your left wan. It's miraculous that whenever he scents a job in front of him, his legs begin to fail him! Then, me bucko, if you lose this chance, you may go an' furrage for yourself!

Jerry. This job'll last for some time too, Captain, an' as soon as the foundations are in, it'll be cushy enough.

Boyle. Won't it be a climbin' job? How d'ye expect me to be able to go up a ladder with these legs? An', if I get up aself, how am I goin' to get down agen?

Mrs. Boyle (viciously). Get wan o' the labourers to carry you down in a hod! You can't climb a laddher, but you can skip like a goat into a snug!

Jerry. I wouldn't let myself be let down that easy, Mr. Boyle; a little exercise, now, might do you all the good in the world.

Boyle. It's a docthor you should have been, Devine— maybe you know more about the pains in me legs than meself that has them?

Jerry (irritated). Oh, I know nothin' about the pains in your legs; I've brought the message that Father Farrell gave me, an' that's all I can do.

Mrs. Boyle. Here, sit down an' take your breakfast, an' go an' get ready; an' don't be actin' as if you couldn't pull a wing out of a dead bee.

Boyle. I want no breakfast, I tell you; it ud choke me afther all that's been said. I've a little spirit left in me still.

Mrs. Boyle. Well, let's see your spirit, then, an' go in at wanst an' put on your moleskin trousers!

Boyle (moving towards the door on left). It ud be b"er for a man to be dead! U-ugh! There's another twinge in me other leg! Nobody but meself knows the sufferin' I'm goin' through with the pains in these legs o' mine!

[*He goes into the room on left as Mary comes out with her hat in her hand.*

Mrs. Boyle. I'll have to push off now, for I'm terrible late already, but I was determined to stay an' hunt that Joxer this time. [*She goes off.*

Jerry. Are you going out, Mary?

Mary. It looks like it when I'm putting on my hat, doesn't it?

Jerry. The bitther word agen, Mary.

Mary. You won't allow me to be friendly with you; if I thry, you deliberately misundherstand it.

Jerry. I didn't always misundherstand it; you were often delighted to have the arms of Jerry around you.

Mary. If you go on talkin' like this, Jerry Devine, you'll make me hate you!

Jerry. Well, let it be either a weddin' or a wake! Listen, Mary, I'm standin' for the Secretaryship of our Union. There's only one opposin' me; I'm popular with all the men, an' a good speaker—all are sayin' that I'll get elected.

Mary. Well?

Jerry. The job's worth three hundred an' fifty pounds a year, Mary. You an' I could live nice an' cosily on that; it would lift you out o' this place an' . . .

Mary. I haven't time to listen to you now—I have to go. [*She is going out, when* Jerry *bars the way.*

Jerry (appealingly). Mary, what's come over you with me for the last few weeks? You hardly speak to me, an' then only a word with a face o' bittherness on it. Have you forgotten, Mary, all the happy evenin's that were as sweet as the scented hawthorn that sheltered the sides o' the road as we saunthered through the country?

Mary. That's all over now. When you get your new job, Jerry, you won't be long findin' a girl far betther than I am for your sweetheart.

Jerry. Never, never, Mary! No matther what happens, you'll always be the same to me.

Mary. I must be off; please let me go, Jerry.

Jerry. I'll go a bit o' the way with you.

Mary. You needn't, thanks; I want to be by meself.

Jerry (*catching her arm*). You're goin' to meet another fella; you've clicked with someone else, me lady!

Mary. That's no concern o' yours, Jerry Devine; let me go!

Jerry. I saw yous comin' out o' the Cornflower Dance Class, an' you hangin' on his arm—a thin, lanky strip of a Micky Dazzler, with a walkin'-stick an' gloves!

Voice of Johnny (*loudly*). What are you doin' there—pullin' about everything!

Voice of Boyle (*loudly and viciously*). I'm puttin' on me moleskin trousers!

Mary. You're hurtin' me arm! Let me go, or I'll scream, an' then you'll have the oul' fella out on top of us!

Jerry. Don't be so hard on a fella, Mary, don't be so hard.

Boyle (*appearing at the door*). What's the meanin' of all this hillabaloo?

Mary. Let me go, let me go!

Boyle. D'ye hear me—what's all this hillabaloo about?

Jerry (*plaintively*). Will you not give us one kind word, one kind word, Mary?

Boyle. D'ye hear me talkin' to yous? What's all this hillabaloo for?

Jerry. Let me kiss your hand, your little, tiny, white hand!

Boyle. Your little, tiny, white hand—are you takin' leave o' your senses, man?

[*Mary breaks away and rushes out.*

Boyle. This is nice goin's on in front of her father!

Jerry. Ah, dhry up, for God's sake!   [*He follows Mary.*

Boyle. Chiselurs don't care a damn now about their parents, they're bringin' their fathers' grey hairs down with sorra to the grave, an' laughin' at it, laughin' at it. Ah, I suppose it's just the same everywhere—the whole worl's in a state o' chassis! (*He sits by the fire*) Breakfast! Well, they can

keep their breakfast for me.   Not if they went down on their
bended knees would I take it—I'll show them I've a little
spirit left in me still! (*He goes over to the press, takes out a plate
and looks at it*) Sassige!   Well, let her keep her sassige. (*He
returns to the fire, takes up the teapot and gives it a gentle shake*)
The tea's wet right enough.

> [*A pause; he rises, goes to the press, takes out the sausage,
>   puts it on the pan, and puts both on the fire.   He attends
>   the sausage with a fork.*

Boyle (*singing*):

When the robins nest agen,

And the flowers are in bloom,

When the Springtime's sunny smile seems to banish all
   sorrow an' gloom;

Then me bonny blue-ey'd lad, if me heart be true till then—

He's promised he'll come back to me,

When the robins nest agen!

> [*He lifts his head at the high note, and then drops his eyes
>   to the pan.*

Boyle (*singing*):

When the . . .

> [*Steps are heard approaching; he whips the pan off the fire
>   and puts it under the bed, then sits down at the fire.   The
>   door opens and a bearded man looking in says:*

You don't happen to want a sewin' machine?

Boyle (*furiously*).   No, I don't want e'er a sewin' machine!

> [*He returns the pan to the fire, and commences to sing again.*

Boyle (*singing*):

When the robins nest agen,

And the flowers they are in bloom,

He's . . .

> [*A thundering knock is heard at the street door.*

Boyle.   There's a terrible tatheraraa—that's a stranger—
that's nobody belongin' to the house.   [*Another loud knock.*

Joxer (*sticking his head in at the door*). Did ye hear them tatherarahs?

Boyle. Well, Joxer, I'm not deaf.

Johnny (*appearing in his shirt and trousers at the door on left; his face is anxious and his voice is tremulous*). Who's that at the door; who's that at the door? Who gave that knock—d'ye yous hear me—are yous deaf or dhrunk or what?

Boyle (*to* Johnny). How the hell do I know who 'tis? Joxer, stick your head out o' the window an' see.

Joxer. An' mebbe get a bullet in the kisser? Ah, none o' them thricks for Joxer! It's betther to be a coward than a corpse!

Boyle (*looking cautiously out of the window*). It's a fella in a thrench coat.

Johnny. Holy Mary, Mother o' God, I . . .

Boyle. He's goin' away—he must ha' got tired knockin'.

[Johnny *returns to the room on left.*

Boyle. Sit down an' have a cup o' tay, Joxer.

Joxer. I'm afraid the missus ud pop in on us agen before we'd know where we are. Somethin's tellin' me to go at wanst.

Boyle. Don't be superstitious, man; we're Dublin men, an' not boyos that's only afther comin' up from the bog o' Allen—though if she did come in, right enough, we'd be caught like rats in a thrap.

Joxer. An' you know the sort she is—she wouldn't listen to reason—an' wanse bitten twice shy.

Boyle (*going over to the window at back*). If the worst came to the worst, you could dart out here, Joxer; it's only a dhrop of a few feet to the roof of the return room, an' the first minute she goes into dh'other room I'll give you the bend, an' you can slip in an' away.

Joxer (*yielding to the temptation*). Ah, I won't stop very long anyhow. (*Picking up a book from the table*) Whose is the buk?

Boyle. Aw, one o' Mary's; she's always readin' lately—nothin' but thrash, too. There's one I was lookin' at dh'other day: three stories, The Doll's House, Ghosts, an' The Wild Duck—buks only fit for chiselurs!

Joxer. Didja ever rade *Elizabeth, or Th' Exile o' Sibayria?* . . . Ah, it's a darlin' story, a daarlin story!

Boyle. You eat your sassige, an' never min' *Th' Exile o' Sibayria.*

> [*Both sit down;* Boyle *fills out tea, pours gravy on* Joxer's *plate, and keeps the sausage for himself.*

Joxer. What are you wearin' your moleskin trousers for?

Boyle. I have to go to a job, Joxer. Just afther you'd gone, Devine kem runnin' in to tell us that Father Farrell said if I went down to the job that's goin' on in Rathmines I'd get a start.

Joxer. Be the holy, that's good news!

Boyle. How is it good news? I wondher if you were in my condition, would you call it good news?

Joxer. I thought . . .

Boyle. You thought! You think too sudden sometimes, Joxer. D'ye know, I'm hardly able to crawl with the pains in me legs!

Joxer. Yis, yis; I forgot the pains in your legs. I know you can do nothin' while they're at you.

Boyle. You forgot; I don't think any of yous realize the state I'm in with the pains in my legs. What ud happen if I had to carry a bag o' cement?

Joxer. Ah, any man havin' the like of them pains id be down an' out, down an' out.

Boyle. I wouldn't mind if he had said it to meself; but, no, oh no, he rushes in an' shouts it out in front o' Juno, an' you know what Juno is, Joxer. We all know Devine knows a little more than the rest of us, but he doesn't act as if he did; he's a good boy, sober, able to talk an' all that, but still . . .

Joxer. Oh ay; able to argufy, but still . . .

Boyle. If he's runnin' afther Mary, aself, he's not goin' to be runnin' afther me. Captain Boyle's able to take care of himself. Afther all, I'm not gettin' brought up on Virol. I never heard him usin' a curse; I don't believe he was ever dhrunk in his life—sure he's not like a Christian at all!

Joxer. You're afther takin' the word out o' me mouth—afther all, a Christian's natural, but he's unnatural.

Boyle. His oul' fella was just the same—a Wicklow man.

Joxer. A Wicklow man! That explains the whole thing. I've met many a Wicklow man in me time, but I never met wan that was any good.

Boyle. 'Father Farrell,' says he, 'sent me down to tell you.' Father Farrell! . . . D'ye know, Joxer, I never like to be beholden to any o' the clergy.

Joxer. It's dangerous, right enough.

Boyle. If they do anything for you, they'd want you to be livin' in the Chapel. . . . I'm goin' to tell you somethin', Joxer, that I wouldn't tell to anybody else—the clergy always had too much power over the people in this unfortunate country.

Joxer. You could sing that if you had an air to it!

Boyle (*becoming enthusiastic*). Didn't they prevent the people in '47 from seizin' the corn, an' they starvin'; didn't they down Parnell; didn't they say that hell wasn't hot enough nor eternity long enough to punish the Fenians? We don't forget, we don't forget them things, Joxer. If they've taken everything else from us, Joxer, they've left us our memory.

Joxer (*emotionally*). For mem'ry's the only friend that grief can call its own, that grief . . . can . . . call . . . its own!

Boyle. Father Farrell's beginnin' to take a great intherest in Captain Boyle; because of what Johnny did for his country, says he to me wan day. It's a curious way to reward Johnny be makin' his poor oul' father work. But that's what the clergy want, Joxer—work, work, work for me an' you; havin' us mulin' from mornin' till night, so that they may be in betther fettle when they come hoppin' round for their dues! Job! Well, let him give his job to wan of his hymn-singin', prayer-spoutin', craw-thumpin' Confraternity men!

[*The voice of a coal-block vendor is heard chanting in the
    street.*

Voice of Coal Vendor. Blocks . . . coal-blocks! Blocks
. . . coal-blocks!

Joxer. God be with the young days when you were
steppin' the deck of a manly ship, with the win' blowin' a
hurricane through the masts, an' the only sound you'd hear
was, 'Port your helm!' an' the only answer, 'Port it is, sir!'

Boyle. Them was days, Joxer, them was days. Nothin'
was too hot or too heavy for me then. Sailin' from the Gulf
o' Mexico to the Antanartic Ocean. I seen things, I seen
things, Joxer, that no mortal man should speak about that
knows his Catechism. Ofen, an' ofen, when I was fixed to
the wheel with a marlin-spike, an' the win's blowin' fierce an'
the waves lashin' an' lashin', till you'd think every minute was
goin' to be your last, an' it blowed, an' blowed—blew is the
right word, Joxer, but blowed is what the sailors use. . . .

Joxer. Aw, it's a darlin' word, a daarlin' word.

Boyle. An', as it blowed an' blowed, I ofen looked up at
the sky an' assed meself the question—what is the stars, what
is the stars?

Voice of Coal Vendor. Any blocks, coal-blocks; blocks,
coal-blocks!

Joxer. Ah, that's the question, that's the question—what
is the stars?

Boyle. An' then, I'd have another look, an' I'd ass meself
—what is the moon?

Joxer. Ah, that's the question—what is the moon, what
is the moon?

[*Rapid steps are heard coming towards the door. Boyle
    makes desperate efforts to hide everything; Joxer rushes to
    the window in a frantic effort to get out; Boyle begins
    to innocently lilt 'Oh, me darlin' Jennie, I will be thrue
    to thee', when the door is opened, and the black face of the
    Coal Vendor appears.*

The Coal Vendor. D'yez want any blocks?

Boyle (with a roar). No, we don't want any blocks!

Joxer (coming back with a sigh of relief). That's afther puttin' the heart across me—I could ha' sworn it was Juno. I'd betther be goin', Captain; you couldn't tell the minute Juno'd hop in on us.

Boyle. Let her hop in; we may as well have it out first as at last. I've made up me mind—I'm not goin' to do only what she damn well likes.

Joxer. Them sentiments does you credit, Captain; I don't like to say anything as between man an' wife, but I say as a butty, as a butty, Captain, that you've stuck it too long, an' that it's about time you showed a little spunk.

How can a man die betther than facin' fearful odds,
For th' ashes of his fathers an' the temples of his gods?

Boyle. She has her rights—there's no one denyin' it, but haven't I me rights too?

Joxer. Of course you have—the sacred rights o' man!

Boyle. Today, Joxer, there's goin' to be issued a proclamation be me, establishin' an independent Republic, an' Juno'll have to take an oath of allegiance.

Joxer. Be firm, be firm, Captain; the first few minutes'll be the worst: if you gently touch a nettle it'll sting you for your pains; grasp it like a lad of mettle, an' as soft as silk remains!

Voice of Juno outside. Can't stop, Mrs. Madigan—I haven't a minute!

Joxer (flying out of the window). Holy God, here she is!

Boyle (packing the things away with a rush in the press). I knew that fella ud stop till she was in on top of us!

[*He sits down by the fire.*
[*Juno enters hastily; she is flurried and excited.*

Juno. Oh, you're in—you must have been only afther comin' in?

Boyle.   No, I never went out.

Juno.   It's curious, then, you never heard the knockin'.

[*She puts her coat and hat on bed.*

Boyle.   Knockin'?   Of course I heard the knockin'.

Juno.   An' why didn't you open the door, then?   I suppose you were so busy with Joxer that you hadn't time.

Boyle.   I haven't seen Joxer since I seen him before.   Joxer! What ud bring Joxer here?

Juno.   D'ye mean to tell me that the pair of yous wasn't collogin' together here when me back was turned?

Boyle.   What ud we be collogin' together about?   I have somethin' else to think of besides collogin' with Joxer.   I can swear on all the holy prayer-books . . .

Mrs. Boyle.   That you weren't in no snug!   Go on in at wanst now, an' take off that moleskin trousers o' yours, an' put on a collar an' tie to smarten yourself up a bit.   There's a visitor comin' with Mary in a minute, an' he has great news for you.

Boyle.   A job, I suppose; let us get wan first before we start lookin' for another.

Mrs. Boyle.   That's the thing that's able to put the win' up you.   Well, it's no job, but news that'll give you the chance o' your life.

Boyle.   What's all the mysthery about?

Mrs. Boyle.   G'win an' take off the moleskin trousers when you're told!   [*Boyle goes into room on left.*

[*Mrs. Boyle tidies up the room, puts the shovel under the bed, and goes to the press.*

Mrs. Boyle.   Oh, God bless us, looka the way everything's thrun about!   Oh, Joxer was here, Joxer was here!

[*Mary enters with Charlie Bentham; he is a young man of twenty-five, tall, good-looking, with a very high opinion of himself generally.   He is dressed in a brown coat, brown knee-breeches, grey stockings, a brown sweater, with a deep blue tie; he carries gloves and a walking-stick.*

Mrs. Boyle (fussing round). Come in, Mr. Bentham; sit down, Mr. Bentham, in this chair; it's more comfortabler than that, Mr. Bentham. Himself'll be here in a minute; he's just takin' off his trousers.

Mary. Mother!

Bentham. Please don't put yourself to any trouble, Mrs. Boyle—I'm quite all right here, thank you.

Mrs. Boyle. An' to think of you knowin' Mary, an' she knowin' the news you had for us, an' wouldn't let on; but it's all the more welcomer now, for we were on our last lap!

Voice of Johnny inside. What are you kickin' up all the racket for?

Boyle (roughly). I'm takin' off me moleskin trousers!

Johnny. Can't you do it, then, without lettin' th' whole house know you're takin' off your trousers? What d'ye want puttin' them on an' takin' them off again?

Boyle. Will you let me alone, will you let me alone? Am I never goin' to be done thryin' to please th' whole o' yous?

Mrs. Boyle (to Bentham). You must excuse th' state o' th' place, Mr. Bentham; th' minute I turn me back that man o' mine always makes a litther o' th' place, a litther o' th' place.

Bentham. Don't worry, Mrs. Boyle; it's all right, I assure . . .

Boyle (inside). Where's me braces; where in th' name o' God did I leave me braces? . . . Ay, did you see where I put me braces?

Johnny (inside, calling out). Ma, will you come in here an' take da away ou' o' this or he'll dhrive me mad.

Mrs. Boyle (going towards the door). Dear, dear, dear, that man'll be lookin' for somethin' on th' day o' Judgement. *(Looking into room and calling to* Boyle) Look at your braces, man, hangin' round your neck!

Boyle (inside). Aw, Holy God!

Mrs. Boyle (calling). Johnny, Johnny, come out here for a minute.

Johnny. Ah, leave Johnny alone, an' don't be annoyin' him!

Mrs. Boyle. Come on, Johnny, till I inthroduce you to Mr. Bentham. (*To* Bentham) My son, Mr. Bentham; he's afther goin' through the mill. He was only a chiselur of a Boy Scout in Easter Week, when he got hit in the hip; and his arm was blew off in the fight in O'Connell Street. (*Johnny comes in.*) Here he is, Mr. Bentham; Mr. Bentham, Johnny. None can deny he done his bit for Irelan', if that's goin' to do him any good.

Johnny (boastfully). I'd do it agen, ma, I'd do it agen; for a principle's a principle.

Mrs. Boyle. Ah, you lost your best principle, me boy, when you lost your arm; them's the only sort o' principles that's any good to a workin' man.

Johnny. Ireland only half free'll never be at peace while she has a son left to pull a trigger.

Mrs. Boyle. To be sure, to be sure—no bread's a lot betther than half a loaf. (*Calling loudly in to* Boyle) Will you hurry up there?

[Boyle *enters in his best trousers, which aren't too good, and looks very uncomfortable in his collar and tie.*

Mrs. Boyle. This is my husband; Mr. Boyle, Mr. Bentham.

Bentham. Ah, very glad to know you, Mr. Boyle. How are you?

Boyle. Ah, I'm not too well at all; I suffer terrible with pains in me legs. Juno can tell you there what . . .

Mrs. Boyle. You won't have many pains in your legs when you hear what Mr. Bentham has to tell you.

Bentham. Juno! What an interesting name! It reminds one of Homer's glorious story of ancient gods and heroes.

Boyle. Yis, doesn't it? You see, Juno was born an' christened in June; I met her in June; we were married in June, an' Johnny was born in June, so wan day I says to her, 'You should ha' been called Juno,' an' the name stuck to her ever since.

Mrs. Boyle. Here, we can talk o' them things agen; let Mr. Bentham say what he has to say now.

Bentham. Well, Mr. Boyle, I suppose you'll remember a Mr. Ellison of Santry—he's a relative of yours, I think.

Boyle (viciously). Is it that prognosticator an' procrastinator! Of course I remember him.

Bentham. Well, he's dead, Mr. Boyle . . .

Boyle. Sorra many'll go into mournin' for him.

Mrs. Boyle. Wait till you hear what Mr. Bentham has to say, an' then, maybe, you'll change your opinion.

Bentham. A week before he died he sent for me to write his will for him. He told me that there were two only that he wished to leave his property to: his second cousin, Michael Finnegan of Santry, and John Boyle, his first cousin, of Dublin.

Boyle (excitedly). Me, is it me, me?

Bentham. You, Mr. Boyle; I'll read a copy of the will that I have here with me, which has been duly filed in the Court of Probate.

[*He takes a paper from his pocket and reads:*

6th February 1922

This is the last Will and Testament of William Ellison, of Santry, in the County of Dublin. I hereby order and wish my property to be sold and divided as follows:—

£20 to the St. Vincent de Paul Society.

£60 for Masses for the repose of my soul (5s. for each Mass).

The rest of my property to be divided between my first and second cousins.

I hereby appoint Timothy Buckly, of Santry, and Hugh Brierly, of Coolock, to be my Executors.

(Signed)   WILLIAM ELLISON.
             HUGH BRIERLY.
             TIMOTHY BUCKLY.
             CHARLES BENTHAM, N.T.

Boyle (*eagerly*).   An' how much'll be comin' out of it, Mr. Bentham?

Bentham.   The Executors told me that half of the property would be anything between £1500 and £2000.

Mary.   A fortune, father, a fortune!

Johnny.   We'll be able to get out o' this place now, an' go somewhere we're not known.

Mrs. Boyle.   You won't have to trouble about a job for awhile, Jack.

Boyle (*fervently*).   I'll never doubt the goodness o' God agen.

Bentham.   I congratulate you, Mr. Boyle.

[*They shake hands.*

Boyle.   An' now, Mr. Bentham, you'll have to have a wet.

Bentham.   A wet?

Boyle.   A wet—a jar—a boul!

Mrs. Boyle.   Jack, you're speakin' to Mr. Bentham, an' not to Joxer.

Boyle (*solemnly*).   Juno . . . Mary . . . Johnny . . . we'll have to go into mournin' at wanst. . . . I never expected that poor Bill ud die so sudden. . . . Well, we all have to die some day . . . you, Juno, to-day . . . an' me, maybe, to-morrow. . . . It's sad, but it can't be helped. . . . Requiescat in pace . . . or, usin' our oul' tongue like St. Patrick or St. Bridget, Guh sayeree jeea ayera!

Mary.   Oh, father, that's not Rest in Peace; that's God save Ireland.

Boyle.   U-u-ugh, it's all the same—isn't it a prayer? . . . Juno, I'm done with Joxer; he's nothin' but a prognosticator an' a . . .

Joxer (*climbing angrily through the window and bounding into the room*).   You're done with Joxer, are you?   Maybe you thought I'd stop on the roof all the night for you!   Joxer out on the roof with the win' blowin' through him was nothin' to you an' your friend with the collar an' tie!

Mrs. Boyle. What in the name o' God brought you out on the roof; what were you doin' there?

Joxer (ironically). I was dhreamin' I was standin' on the bridge of a ship, an' she sailin' the Antartic Ocean, an' it blowed, an' blowed, an' I lookin' up at the sky an' sayin'; what is the stars, what is the stars?

Mrs. Boyle (opening the door and standing at it). Here, get ou' o' this, Joxer Daly; I was always thinkin' you had a slate off.

Joxer (moving to the door). I have to laugh every time I look at the deep-sea sailor; an' a row on a river ud make him sea-sick!

Boyle. Get ou' o' this before I take the law into me own hands!

Joxer (going out). Say aw rewaeawr, but not good-bye. Lookin' for work, an' prayin' to God he won't get it!

[*He goes.*

Mrs. Boyle. I'm tired tellin' you what Joxer was; maybe now you see yourself the kind he is.

Boyle. He'll never blow the froth off a pint o' mine agen, that's a sure thing. Johnny . . . Mary . . . you're to keep yourselves to yourselves for the future. Juno, I'm done with Joxer. . . . I'm a new man from this out. . . .

[*Clasping* Juno's *hand, and singing emotionally:*

O, me darlin' Juno, I will be thrue to thee;
Me own, me darlin' Juno, you're all the world to me.

CURTAIN

ACT II

The same, but the furniture is more plentiful, and of a vulgar nature. A glaringly upholstered armchair and lounge; cheap pictures and photos everywhere. Every available spot is ornamented with huge vases filled with artificial flowers. Crossed festoons of coloured paper chains stretch from end to end of ceiling. On the table is an old attaché case. It is about six in the evening, and two days after the First Act. Boyle, in his shirt-sleeves, is voluptuously stretched on the sofa; he is smoking a clay pipe. He is half asleep. A lamp is lighting on the table. After a few moments' pause the voice of Joxer is heard singing softly outside at the door—'Me pipe I'll smoke, as I dhrive me moke—are you there, Mor . . . ee . . . ar . . . i . . . tees!'

Boyle (*leaping up, takes a pen in his hand and busies himself with papers*). Come along, Joxer, me son, come along.

Joxer (*putting his head in*). Are you be yourself?

Boyle. Come on, come on; that doesn't matther; I'm masther now, an' I'm goin' to remain masther.

[Joxer *comes in.*

Joxer. How d'ye feel now, as a man o' money?

Boyle (*solemnly*). It's a responsibility, Joxer, a great responsibility.

Joxer. I suppose 'tis now, though you wouldn't think it.

Boyle. Joxer, han' me over that attackey case on the table there. (Joxer *hands the case.*) Ever since the Will was passed I've run hundreds o' dockyments through me han's— I tell you, you have to keep your wits about you.

[He busies himself with papers.

Joxer. Well, I won't disturb you; I'll dhrop in when . . .

Boyle (*hastily*). It's all right, Joxer, this is the last one to be signed to-day. (*He signs a paper, puts it into the case, which*

31

he shuts with a snap, and sits back pompously in the chair.) Now, Joxer, you want to see me; I'm at your service—what can I do for you, me man?

Joxer. I've just dhropped in with the £3:5s. that Mrs. Madigan riz on the blankets an' table for you, an' she says you're to be in no hurry payin' it back.

Boyle. She won't be long without it; I expect the first cheque for a couple o' hundhred any day. There's the five bob for yourself—go on, take it, man; it'll not be the last you'll get from the Captain. Now an' agen we have our differ, but we're there together all the time.

Joxer. Me for you, an' you for me, like the two Musketeers.

Boyle. Father Farrell stopped me to-day an' tole me how glad he was I fell in for the money.

Joxer. He'll be stoppin' you ofen enough now; I suppose it was 'Mr.' Boyle with him?

Boyle. He shuk me be the han' . . .

Joxer (*ironically*). I met with Napper Tandy, an' he shuk me be the han'!

Boyle. You're seldom asthray, Joxer, but you're wrong shipped this time. What you're sayin' of Father Farrell is very near to blasfeemey. I don't like any one to talk disrespectful of Father Farrell.

Joxer. You're takin' me up wrong, Captain; I wouldn't let a word be said agen Father Farrell—the heart o' the rowl, that's what he is; I always said he was a darlin' man, a daarlin' man.

Boyle. Comin' up the stairs who did I meet but that bummer, Nugent. 'I seen you talkin' to Father Farrell,' says he, with a grin on him. 'He'll be folleyin' you,' says he, 'like a Guardian Angel from this out'—all the time the oul' grin on him, Joxer.

Joxer. I never seen him yet but he had that oul' grin on him!

Boyle. 'Mr. Nugent,' says I, 'Father Farrell is a man

o' the people, an', as far as I know the History o' me country, the priests was always in the van of the fight for Irelan's freedom.'

Joxer (fervently):

> Who was it led the van, Soggart Aroon?
> Since the fight first began, Soggart Aroon?

Boyle. 'Who are you tellin'?' says he. 'Didn't they let down the Fenians, an' didn't they do in Parnell? An' now . . .' 'You ought to be ashamed o' yourself,' says I, interruptin' him, 'not to know the History o' your country.' An' I left him gawkin' where he was.

Joxer. Where ignorance 's bliss 'tis folly to be wise; I wondher did he ever read the Story o' Irelan'.

Boyle. Be J. L. Sullivan? Don't you know he didn't.

Joxer. Ah, it's a darlin' buk, a daarlin' buk!

Boyle. You'd betther be goin', now, Joxer; his Majesty, Bentham, 'll be here any minute, now.

Joxer. Be the way things is lookin', it'll be a match between him an' Mary. She's thrun over Jerry altogether. Well, I hope it will, for he's a darlin' man.

Boyle. I'm glad you think so—I don't. (*Irritably*) What's darlin' about him?

Joxer (nonplussed). I only seen him twiced; if you want to know me, come an' live with me.

Boyle. He's too dignified for me—to hear him talk you'd think he knew as much as a Boney's Oraculum. He's given up his job as teacher, an' is goin' to become a solicitor in Dublin—he's been studyin' law. I suppose he thinks I'll set him up, but he's wrong shipped. An' th' other fella— Jerry's as bad. The two o' them ud give you a pain in your face, listenin' to them; Jerry believin' in nothin', an' Bentham believin' in everythin'. One that says all is God an' no man; an' th' other that says all is man an' no God!

Joxer. Well, I'll be off now.

Boyle. Don't forget to dhrop down afther awhile; we'll have a quiet jar, an' a song or two.

Joxer. Never fear.

Boyle. An' tell Mrs. Madigan that I hope we'll have the pleasure of her organization at our little enthertainment.

Joxer. Righto; we'll come down together.   [*He goes out.*

    [Johnny *comes from room on left, and sits down moodily at the fire.* Boyle *looks at him for a few moments, and shakes his head. He fills his pipe.*

Voice of Juno at the door. Open the door, Jack; this thing has me nearly kilt with the weight.

    [Boyle *opens the door.* Juno *enters carrying the box of a gramophone, followed by* Mary *carrying the horn and some parcels.* Juno *leaves the box on the table and flops into a chair.*

Juno. Carryin' that from Henry Street was no joke.

Boyle. U-u-ugh, that's a grand-lookin' insthrument—how much was it?

Juno. Pound down, an' five to be paid at two shillin's a week.

Boyle. That's reasonable enough.

Juno. I'm afraid we're runnin' into too much debt; first the furniture, an' now this.

Boyle. The whole lot won't be much out of £2000.

Mary. I don't know what you wanted a gramophone for—I know Charlie hates them; he says they're destructive of real music.

Boyle. Desthructive of music—that fella ud give you a pain in your face. All a gramophone wants is to be properly played; its thrue wondher is only felt when everythin's quiet—what a gramophone wants is dead silence!

Mary. But, father, Jerry says the same; afther all, you can only appreciate music when your ear is properly trained.

Boyle. That's another fella ud give you a pain in your

face. Properly thrained! I suppose you couldn't appreciate football unless your fut was properly thrained.

Mrs. Boyle (*to* Mary). Go on in ower that an' dress, or Charlie'll be in on you, an' tea nor nothin'll be ready.

[Mary *goes into room left.*

Mrs. Boyle (*arranging table for tea*). You didn't look at our new gramophone, Johnny?

Johnny. 'Tisn't gramophones I'm thinking of.

Mrs. Boyle. An' what is it you're thinkin' of, allanna?

Johnny. Nothin', nothin', nothin'.

Mrs. Boyle. Sure, you must be thinkin' of somethin'; it's yourself that has yourself the way y'are; sleepin' wan night in me sisther's, an' the nex' in your father's brother's—you'll get no rest goin' on that way.

Johnny. I can rest nowhere, nowhere, nowhere.

Mrs. Boyle. Sure, you're not thryin' to rest anywhere.

Johnny. Let me alone, let me alone, let me alone, for God's sake.   [*A knock at street door.*

Mrs. Boyle (*in a flutter*). Here he is; here's Mr. Bentham!

Boyle. Well, there's room for him; it's a pity there's not a brass band to play him in.

Mrs. Boyle. We'll han' the tea round, an' not be clusthered round the table, as if we never seen nothin'.

[*Steps are heard approaching, and* Juno *opening the door, allows* Bentham *to enter.*

Juno. Give your hat an' stick to Jack, there . . . sit down, Mr. Bentham . . . no, not there . . . in th' easy chair be the fire . . . there, that's betther. Mary'll be out to you in a minute.

Boyle (*solemnly*). I seen be the paper this mornin' that Consols was down half per cent. That's serious, min' you, an' shows the whole counthry's in a state o' chassis.

Mrs. Boyle. What's Consols, Jack?

Boyle. Consols? Oh, Consols is—oh, there's no use tellin' women what Consols is—th' wouldn't undherstand.

Bentham. It's just as you were saying, Mr. Boyle . . .

[*Mary enters, charmingly dressed.*

Bentham. Oh, good evening, Mary; how pretty you're looking!

Mary (archly). Am I?

Boyle. We were just talkin' when you kem in, Mary; I was tellin' Mr. Bentham that the whole counthry's in a state o' chassis.

Mary (to Bentham). Would you prefer the green or the blue ribbon round me hair, Charlie?

Mrs. Boyle. Mary, your father's speakin'.

Boyle (rapidly). I was jus' tellin' Mr. Bentham that the whole counthry's in a state o' chassis.

Mary. I'm sure you're frettin', da, whether it is or no.

Mrs. Boyle. With all our churches an' religions, the worl's not a bit the betther.

Boyle (with a commanding gesture). Tay!

[*Mary and* Mrs. Boyle *dispense the tea.*

Mrs. Boyle. An' Irelan's takin' a leaf out o' the worl's buk; when we got the makin' of our own laws I thought we'd never stop to look behind us, but instead of that we never stopped to look before us! If the people ud folley up their religion betther there'd be a betther chance for us—what do you think, Mr. Bentham?

Bentham. I'm afraid I can't venture to express an opinion on that point, Mrs. Boyle; dogma has no attraction for me.

Mrs. Boyle. I forgot you didn't hold with us: what's this you said you were?

Bentham. A Theosophist, Mrs. Boyle.

Mrs. Boyle. An' what in the name o' God's a Theosophist?

Boyle. A Theosophist, Juno, 's a—tell her, Mr. Bentham. tell her.

Bentham. It's hard to explain in a few words: Theosophy's founded on The Vedas, the religious books of the East. Its central theme is the existence of an all-pervading Spirit—

the Life-Breath. Nothing really exists but this one Universal Life-Breath. And whatever even seems to exist separately from this Life-Breath, doesn't really exist at all. It is all vital force in man, in all animals, and in all vegetation. This Life-Breath is called the Prawna.

Mrs. Boyle. The Prawna! What a comical name!

Boyle. Prawna; yis, the Prawna. (*Blowing gently through his lips*) That's the Prawna!

Mrs. Boyle. Whist, whist, Jack.

Bentham. The happiness of man depends upon his sympathy with this Spirit. Men who have reached a high state of excellence are called Yogi. Some men become Yogi in a short time, it may take others millions of years.

Boyle. Yogi! I seen hundhreds of them in the streets o' San Francisco.

Bentham. It is said by these Yogi that if we practise certain mental exercises we would have powers denied to others— for instance, the faculty of seeing things that happen miles and miles away.

Mrs. Boyle. I wouldn't care to meddle with that sort o' belief; it's a very curious religion, altogether.

Boyle. What's curious about it? Isn't all religions curious? —if they weren't, you wouldn't get any one to believe them. But religions is passin' away—they've had their day like everything else. Take the real Dublin people, f'rinstance: they know more about Charlie Chaplin an' Tommy Mix than they do about SS. Peter an' Paul!

Mrs. Boyle. You don't believe in ghosts, Mr. Bentham?

Mary. Don't you know he doesn't, mother?

Bentham. I don't know that, Mary. Scientists are beginning to think that what we call ghosts are sometimes seen by person of a certain nature. They say that sensational actions, such as the killing of a person, demand great energy, and that energy lingers in the place where the action occurred. People may live in the place and see nothing, when someone may come along whose personality has some peculiar connection with the energy of the place, and, in a flash, the person sees the whole affair.

Johnny (*rising swiftly, pale and affected*). What sort o' talk is this to be goin' on with? Is there nothin' better to be talkin' about but the killin' o' people? My God, isn't it bad enough for these things to happen without talkin' about them!   [*He hurriedly goes into the room on left.*

Bentham. Oh, I'm very sorry, Mrs. Boyle; I never thought . . .

Mrs. Boyle (*apologetically*). Never mind, Mr. Bentham, he's very touchy.

[*A frightened scream is heard from* Johnny *inside.*

Mrs. Boyle. Mother of God, what's that?

[*He rushes out again, his face pale, his lips twitching, his limbs trembling.*

Johnny. Shut the door, shut the door, quick, for God's sake! Great God, have mercy on me! Blessed Mother o' God, shelter me, shelther your son!

Mrs. Boyle (*catching him in her arms*). What's wrong with you? What ails you? Sit down, sit down, here, on the bed . . . there now . . . there now.

Mary. Johnny, Johnny, what ails you?

Johnny. I seen him, I seen him . . . kneelin' in front o' the statue . . . merciful Jesus, have pity on me!

Mrs. Boyle (*to* Boyle). Get him a glass o' whisky . . . quick, man, an' don't stand gawkin'.   [Boyle *gets the whisky.*

Johnny. Sit here, sit here, mother . . . between me an' the door.

Mrs. Boyle. I'll sit beside you as long as you like, only tell me what was it came across you at all?

Johnny (*after taking some drink*). I seen him. . . . I seen Robbie Tancred kneelin' down before the statue . . . an' the red light shinin' on him . . . an' when I went in . . . he turned an' looked at me . . . an' I seen the woun's bleedin'

in his breast. . . . Oh, why did he look at me like that? . . .
it wasn't my fault that he was done in. . . . Mother o' God,
keep him away from me!

Mrs. Boyle. There, there, child, you've imagined it all.
There was nothin' there at all—it was the red light you seen,
an' the talk we had put all the rest into your head. Here,
dhrink more o' this—it'll do you good. . . . An', now, stretch
yourself down on the bed for a little. (*To* Boyle) Go in,
Jack, an' show him it was only in his own head it was.

Boyle (*making no move*). E-e-e-e-eh; it's all nonsense; it
was only a shadda he saw.

Mary. Mother o' God, he made me heart lep!

Bentham. It was simply due to an overwrought imagina-
tion—we all get that way at times.

Mrs. Boyle. There, dear, lie down in the bed, an' I'll put
the quilt across you . . . e-e-e-eh, that's it . . . you'll be
as right as the mail in a few minutes.

Johnny. Mother, go into the room an' see if the light's
lightin' before the statue.

Mrs. Boyle (*to* Boyle). Jack, run in an' see if the light's
lightin' before the statue.

Boyle (*to* Mary). Mary, slip in an' see if the light's lightin'
before the statue.   [*Mary hesitates to go in.*

Bentham. It's all right; Mary, I'll go.

    [*He goes into the room; remains for a few moments, and
    returns.*

Bentham. Everything's just as it was—the light burning
bravely before the statue.

Boyle. Of course; I knew it was all nonsense.

                        [*A knock at the door.*

Boyle (*going to open the door*). E-e-e-e-eh.

    [*He opens it, and* Joxer, *followed by* Mrs. Madigan, *enters.*
    Mrs. Madigan *is a strong, dapper little woman of about
    forty-five; her face is almost always a widespread smile
    of complacency. She is a woman who, in manner at least,*

*can mourn with them that mourn, and rejoice with them
that do rejoice. When she is feeling comfortable, she is
inclined to be reminiscent; when others say anything, or
following a statement made by herself, she has a habit
of putting her head a little to one side, and nodding it
rapidly several times in succession, like a bird pecking at
a hard berry. Indeed, she has a good deal of the bird in
her, but the bird instinct is by no means a melodious
one. She is ignorant, vulgar and forward, but her heart
is generous withal. For instance, she would help a
neighbour's sick child; she would probably kill the
child, but her intention would be to cure it; she would
be more at home helping a drayman to lift a fallen horse.
She is dressed in a rather soiled grey dress and a vivid
purple blouse; in her hair is a huge comb, ornamented with
huge coloured beads. She enters with a gliding step,
beaming smile and nodding head. Boyle receives them
effusively.*

Boyle. Come on in, Mrs. Madigan; come on in; I was
afraid you weren't comin'. . . . (*Slyly*) There's some people
able to dhress, ay, Joxer?

Joxer. Fair as the blossoms that bloom in the May, an'
sweet as the scent of the new-mown hay. . . . Ah, well she
may wear them.

Mrs. Madigan (looking at Mary). I know some as are as
sweet as the blossoms that bloom in the May—oh, no names,
no pack dhrill !

Boyle. An' now I'll inthroduce the pair o' yous to Mary's
intended : Mr. Bentham, this is Mrs. Madigan, an oul'
back-parlour neighbour, that, if she could help it at all, ud
never see a body shuk !

Bentham (rising, and tentatively shaking the hand of Mrs.
Madigan). I'm sure, it's a great pleasure to know you, Mrs.
Madigan.

Mrs. Madigan. An' I'm goin' to tell you, Mr. Bentham,

you're goin' to get as nice a bit o' skirt in Mary, there, as ever you seen in your puff. Not like some of the dhressed-up dolls that's knockin' about lookin' for men when it's a skelpin' they want. I remember, as well as I remember yestherday, the day she was born—of a Tuesday, the 25th o' June, in the year 1901, at thirty-three minutes past wan in the day be Foley's clock, the pub at the corner o' the street. A cowld day it was too, for the season o' the year, an' I remember sayin' to Joxer, there, who I met comin' up th' stairs, that the new arrival in Boyle's ud grow up a hardy chiselur if it lived, an' that she'd be somethin' one o' these days that nobody suspected, an' so signs on it, here she is to-day, goin' to be married to a young man lookin' as if he'd be fit to commensurate in any position in life it ud please God to call him!

Boyle (effusively). Sit down, Mrs. Madigan, sit down, me oul' sport. (*To* Bentham) This is Joxer Daly, Past Chief Ranger of the Dear Little Shamrock Branch of the Irish National Foresters, an oul' front-top neighbour, that never despaired, even in the darkest days of Ireland's sorra.

Joxer. Nil desperandum, Captain, nil desperandum.

Boyle. Sit down, Joxer, sit down. The two of us was ofen in a tight corner.

Mrs. Boyle. Ay, in Foley's snug!

Joxer. An' we kem out of it flyin', we kem out of it flyin', Captain.

Boyle. An' now for a dhrink—I know yous won't refuse an oul' friend.

Mrs. Madigan (to Juno). Is Johnny not well, Mrs. . . . .

Mrs. Boyle (warningly). S-s-s-sh.

Mrs. Madigan. Oh, the poor darlin'.

Boyle. Well, Mrs. Madigan, is it tea or what?

Mrs. Madigan. Well, speakin' for meself, I jus' had me tea a minute ago, an' I'm afraid to dhrink any more—I'm never the same when I dhrink too much tay. Thanks, all the same, Mr. Boyle.

Boyle. Well, what about a bottle o' stout or a dhrop o' whisky?

Mrs. Madigan. A bottle o' stout ud be a little too heavy for me stummock afther me tay. . . . A-a-ah, I'll thry the ball o' malt.   [*Boyle prepares the whisky.*

Mrs. Madigan. There's nothin' like a ball o' malt occasional like—too much of it isn't good. (*To* Boyle, *who is adding water*) Ah, God, Johnny, don't put too much wather on it! (*She drinks.*) I suppose yous'll be lavin' this place.

Boyle. I'm looking for a place near the sea; I'd like the place that you might say was me cradle, to be me grave as well. The sea is always callin' me.

Joxer. She is callin', callin', callin', in the win' an' on the sea.

Boyle. Another dhrop o' whisky, Mrs. Madigan?

Mrs. Madigan. Well, now, it ud be hard to refuse seein' the suspicious times that's in it.

Boyle (*with a commanding gesture*). Song! . . . Juno . . . Mary . . . 'Home to Our Mountains'!

Mrs. Madigan (*enthusiastically*). Hear, hear!

Joxer. Oh, tha's a darlin' song, a daarlin' song!

Mary (*bashfully*). Ah no, da; I'm not in a singin' humour.

Mrs. Madigan. Gawn with you, child, an' you only goin' to be marrid; I remember as well as I remember yestherday, —it was on a lovely August evenin', exactly, accordin' to date, fifteen years ago, come the Tuesday folleyin' the nex' that's comin' on, when me own man—*the Lord be good to him*— an' me was sittin' shy together in a doty little nook on a counthry road, adjacent to The Stiles. 'That'll scratch your lovely, little white neck,' says he, ketchin' hould of a danglin' bramble branch, holdin' clusters of the loveliest flowers you ever seen, an' breakin' it off, so that his arm fell, accidental like, roun' me waist, an' as I felt it tightenin', an' tightenin', an' tightenin', I thought me buzzom was every minute goin' to burst out into a roystherin' song about

'The little green leaves that were shakin' on the threes,
The gallivantin' buttherflies, an' buzzin' o' the bees!'

Boyle. Ordher for the song!

Juno. Come on, Mary—we'll do our best.

[*Juno and Mary stand up, and choosing a suitable position, sing simply 'Home to Our Mountains'.*

[*They bow to the company, and return to their places.*

Boyle (*emotionally, at the end of song*). Lull . . . me . . . to . . . rest!

Joxer (*clapping his hands*). Bravo, bravo! Darlin' girulls, darlin' girulls!

Mrs. Madigan. Juno, I never seen you in betther form.

Bentham. Very nicely rendered indeed.

Mrs. Madigan. A noble call, a noble call!

Mrs. Boyle. What about yourself, Mrs. Madigan?

[*After some coaxing,* Mrs. Madigan *rises, and in a quavering voice sings the following verse:*

If I were a blackbird I'd whistle and sing;
I'd follow the ship that my thrue love was in;
An' on the top riggin', I'd there build me nest,
An' at night I would sleep on me Willie's white breast!

[*Becoming husky, amid applause, she sits down.*

Mrs. Madigan. Ah, me voice is too husky now, Juno; though I remember the time when Maisie Madigan could sing like a nightingale at matin' time. I remember as well as I remember yesterday, at a party given to celebrate the comin' of the first chiselur to Annie an' Benny Jimeson—who was the barber, yous may remember, in Henrietta Street, that, afther Easter Week, hung out a green, white an' orange pole, an' then, when the Tans started their Jazz dancin', whipped it in agen, an' stuck out a red, white an' blue wan instead, givin' as an excuse that a barber's pole was strictly non-political—singin' 'An' You'll Remember Me' with the top notes quiverin' in a dead hush of pethrified attention, folleyed be a clappin' o' han's that shuk the tumblers on the table, an' capped by Jimeson, the barber, sayin' that it was the best rendherin' of 'You'll Remember Me' he ever heard in his natural!

Boyle (*peremptorily*). Ordher for Joxer's song!

Joxer. Ah no, I couldn't; don't ass me, Captain.

Boyle. Joxer's song, Joxer's song—give us wan of your shut-eyed wans.

> [Joxer *settles himself in his chair; takes a drink; clears his throat; solemnly closes his eyes, and begins to sing in a very querulous voice:*

She is far from the lan' where her young hero sleeps,
An' lovers around her are sighing   [*He hesitates.*
An' lovers around her are sighin' . . . sighin' . . . sighin' . . .   [*A pause.*

Boyle (*imitating* Joxer):

And lovers around her are sighing!

What's the use of you thryin' to sing the song if you don't know it?

Mary. Thry another one, Mr. Daly—maybe you'd be more fortunate.

Mrs. Madigan. Gawn, Joxer; thry another wan.

Joxer (*starting again*):

I have heard the mavis singin' his love song to the morn;
I have seen the dew-dhrop clingin' to the rose jus' newly born; but . . . but . . . (*frantically*) To the rose jus' newly born . . . newly born . . . born.

Johnny. Mother, put on the gramophone, for God's sake, an' stop Joxer's bawlin'.

Boyle (*commandingly*). Gramophone! . . . I hate to see fellas thryin' to do what they're not able to do.

> [Boyle *arranges the gramophone, and is about to start it, when voices are heard of persons descending the stairs.*

Mrs. Boyle (warningly). Whisht, Jack, don't put it on, don't put it on yet; this must be poor Mrs. Tancred comin' down to go to the hospital—I forgot all about them bringin' the body to the church to-night. Open the door, Mary, an' give them a bit o' light.

[*Mary opens the door, and* Mrs. Tancred—*a very old woman, obviously shaken by the death of her son—appears, accompanied by several neighbours. The first few phrases are spoken before they appear.*

First Neighbour. It's a sad journey we're goin' on, but God's good, an' the Republicans won't be always down.

Mrs. Tancred. Ah, what good is that to me now? Whether they're up or down—it won't bring me darlin' boy from the grave.

Mrs. Boyle. Come in an' have a hot cup o' tay, Mrs. Tancred, before you go.

Mrs. Tancred. Ah, I can take nothin' now, Mrs. Boyle— I won't be long afther him.

First Neighbour. Still an' all, he died a noble death, an' we'll bury him like a king.

Mrs. Tancred. An' I'll go on livin' like a pauper. Ah, what's the pains I suffered bringin' him into the world to carry him to his cradle, to the pains I'm sufferin' now, carryin' him out o' the world to bring him to his grave!

Mary. It would be better for you not to go at all, Mrs. Tancred, but to stay at home beside the fire with some o' the neighbours.

Mrs. Tancred. I seen the first of him, an' I'll see the last of him.

Mrs. Boyle. You'd want a shawl, Mrs. Tancred; it's a cowld night, an' the win's blowin' sharp.

Mrs. Madigan (rushing out). I've a shawl above.

Mrs. Tancred. Me home is gone now; he was me only child, an' to think that he was lyin' for a whole night stretched out on the side of a lonely counthry lane, with his head, his

darlin' head, that I ofen kissed an' fondled, half hidden in the
wather of a runnin' brook.   An' I'm told he was the leadher
of the ambush where me nex' door neighbour, Mrs. Mannin',
lost her Free State soldier son.   An' now here's the two of us
oul' women, standin' one on each side of a scales o' sorra,
balanced be the bodies of our two dead darlin' sons.   (Mrs.
Madigan *returns, and wraps a shawl around her.*)   God bless
you, Mrs. Madigan. . . . (*She moves slowly towards the door*)
Mother o' God, Mother o' God, have pity on the pair of us!
. . . O Blessed Virgin, where were you when me darlin' son
was riddled with bullets, when me darlin' son was riddled with
bullets! . . . Sacred Heart of the Crucified Jesus, take away
our hearts o' stone . . . an' give us hearts o' flesh! . . .
Take away this murdherin' hate . . . an' give us Thine own
eternal love!   [*They pass out of the room.*

Mrs. Boyle (*explanatorily to* Bentham).   That was Mrs.
Tancred of the two-pair back; her son was found, e'er
yestherday, lyin' out beyant Finglas riddled with bullets.   A
Die-hard he was, be all accounts.   He was a nice quiet boy,
but lattherly he went to hell, with his Republic first, an'
Republic last an' Republic over all.   He often took tea with
us here, in the oul' days, an' Johnny, there, an' him used to be
always together.

Johnny.   Am I always to be havin' to tell you that he was
no friend o' mine?   I never cared for him, an' he could never
stick me.   It's not because he was Commandant of the
Battalion that I was Quarther-Masther of, that we were friends.

Mrs. Boyle.   He's gone now—the Lord be good to him!
God help his poor oul' creature of a mother, for no matther
whose friend or enemy he was, he was her poor son.

Bentham.   The whole thing is terrible, Mrs. Boyle; but
the only way to deal with a mad dog is to destroy him.

Mrs. Boyle.   An' to think of me forgettin' about him bein'
brought to the church to-night, an' we singin' an' all, but it
was well we hadn't the gramophone goin', anyhow.

Boyle. Even if we had aself. We've nothin' to do with these things, one way or t'other. That's the Government's business, an' let them do what we're payin' them for doin'.

Mrs. Boyle. I'd like to know how a body's not to mind these things; look at the way they're afther leavin' the people in this very house. Hasn't the whole house, nearly, been massacreed? There's young Dougherty's husband with his leg off; Mrs. Travers that had her son blew up be a mine in Inchegeela, in Co. Cork; Mrs. Mannin' that lost wan of her sons in an ambush a few weeks ago, an' now, poor Mrs. Tancred's only child gone west with his body made a collandher of. Sure, if it's not our business, I don't know whose business it is.

Boyle. Here, there, that's enough about them things; they don't affect us, an' we needn't give a damn. If they want a wake, well, let them have a wake. When I was a sailor, I was always resigned to meet with a wathery grave; an' if they want to be soldiers, well, there's no use o' them squealin' when they meet a soldier's fate.

Joxer. Let me like a soldier fall—me breast expandin' to th' ball!

Mrs. Boyle. In wan way, she deserves all she got; for lately, she let th' Die-hards make an open house of th' place; an' for th' last couple of months, either when th' sun was risin' or when th' sun was settin', you had C.I.D. men burstin' into your room, assin' you where were you born, where were you christened, where were you married, an' where would you be buried!

Johnny. For God's sake, let us have no more o' this talk.

Mrs. Madigan. What about Mr. Boyle's song before we start th' gramophone?

Mary (*getting her hat, and putting it on*). Mother, Charlie and I are goin' out for a little sthroll.

Mrs. Boyle. All right, darlin'.

Bentham (*going out with* Mary). We won't be long away, Mrs. Boyle.

Mrs. Madigan. Gwan, Captain, gwan.

Boyle. E-e-e-e-eh, I'd want to have a few more jars in me, before I'd be in settle for singin'.

Joxer. Give us that poem you writ t'other day. (*To the rest*) Aw, it's a darlin' poem, a daarlin' poem.

Mrs. Boyle. God bless us, is he startin' to write poetry!

Boyle (*rising to his feet*). E-e-e-e-eh.

[*He recites in an emotional, consequential manner the following verses:*

Shawn an' I were friends, sir, to me he was all in all.

His work was very heavy and his wages were very small.

None betther on th' beach as Docker, I'll go bail,

'Tis now I'm feelin' lonely, for to-day he lies in jail.

He was not what some call pious—seldom at church or
    prayer;

For the greatest scoundrels I know, sir, goes every
    Sunday there.

Fond of his pint—well, rather, but hated the Boss by
    creed

But never refused a copper to comfort a pal in need.

E-e-e-e-eh.   [*He sits down.*

Mrs. Madigan. Grand, grand; you should folly that up, you should folly that up.

Joxer. It's a daarlin' poem!

Boyle (*delightedly*). E-e-e-e-eh.

Johnny. Are yous goin' to put on th' gramophone to-night, or are yous not?

Mrs. Boyle. Gwan, Jack, put on a record.

Mrs. Madigan. Gwan, Captain, gwan.

Boyle. Well, yous'll want to keep a dead silence.

[*He sets a record, starts the machine, and it begins to play
    'If you're Irish, come into the Parlour'. As the tune
    is in full blare, the door is suddenly opened by a brisk,
    little bald-headed man, dressed circumspectly in a black*

suit; he glares fiercely at all in the room; he is 'Needle Nugent', a tailor. He carries his hat in his hand.

Nugent (loudly, above the noise of the gramophone). Are yous goin' to have that thing bawlin' an' the funeral of Mrs. Tancred's son passin' the house? Have none of yous any respect for the Irish people's National regard for the dead?

[*Boyle stops the gramophone.*

Mrs. Boyle. Maybe, Needle Nugent, it's nearly time we had a little less respect for the dead, an' a little more regard for the livin'.

Mrs. Madigan. We don't want you, Mr. Nugent, to teach us what we learned at our mother's knee. You don't look yourself as if you were dyin' of grief; if y'ass Maisie Madigan anything, I'd call you a real thrue Die-hard an' live-soft Republican, attendin' Republican funerals in the day, an' stoppin' up half the night makin' suits for the Civic Guards!

[*Persons are heard running down to the street, some saying, 'Here it is, here it is.' Nugent withdraws, and the rest, except* Johnny, *go to the window looking into the street, and look out. Sounds of a crowd coming nearer are heard; portion are singing:*

> To Jesus' Heart all burning
> With fervent love for men,
> My heart with fondest yearning
> Shall raise its joyful strain.
> While ages course along,
> Blest be with loudest song
> The Sacred Heart of Jesus
> By every heart and tongue.

Mrs. Boyle. Here's the hearse, here's the hearse!

Boyle. There's t'oul' mother walkin' behin' the coffin.

Mrs. Madigan. You can hardly see the coffin with the wreaths.

Joxer. Oh, it's a darlin' funeral, a daarlin' funeral!

Mrs. Madigan. W'd have a betther view from the street.

Boyle. Yes—this place ud give you a crick in your neck.

> [*They leave the room, and go down.* Johnny *sits moodily by the fire.*

> [*A young man enters; he looks at* Johnny *for a moment.*

The Young Man. Quarther-Masther Boyle.

Johnny (with a start). The Mobilizer!

The Young Man. You're not at the funeral?

Johnny. I'm not well.

The Young Man. I'm glad I've found you; you were stoppin' at your aunt's; I called there but you'd gone. I've to give you an ordher to attend a Battalion Staff meetin' the night afther to-morrow.

Johnny. Where?

The Young Man. I don't know; you're to meet me at the Pillar at eight o'clock; then we're to go to a place I'll be told of to-night; there we'll meet a mothor that'll bring us to the meeting. They think you might be able to know somethin' about them that gave the bend where Commandant Tancred was shelterin'.

Johnny. I'm not goin', then. I know nothing about Tancred.

The Young Man (at the door). You'd betther come for your own sake—remember your oath.

Johnny (passionately). I won't go! Haven't I done enough for Ireland! I've lost me arm, an' me hip's desthroyed so that I'll never be able to walk right agen! Good God, haven't I done enough for Ireland?

The Young Man. Boyle, no man can do enough for Ireland!

> [*He goes.*

> [*Faintly in the distance the crowd is heard saying:*

Hail, Mary, full of grace, the Lord is with Thee; Blessed art Thou amongst women, and blessed, etc.

CURTAIN

ACT III

The same as Act II. It is about half-past six on a November evening; a bright fire burns in the grate; Mary, dressed to go out, is sitting on a chair by the fire, leaning forward, her hands under her chin, her elbows on her knees. A look of dejection, mingled with uncertain anxiety, is on her face. A lamp, turned low, is lighting on the table. The votive light under the picture of the Virgin gleams more redly than ever. Mrs. Boyle is putting on her hat and coat. It is two months later.

Mrs. Boyle. An' has Bentham never even written to you since—not one line for the past month?

Mary (tonelessly). Not even a line, mother.

Mrs. Boyle. That's very curious. . . . What came between the two of yous at all? To leave you so sudden, an' yous so great together. . . . To go away t' England, an' not to even leave you his address. . . . The way he was always bringin' you to dances, I thought he was mad afther you. Are you sure you said nothin' to him?

Mary. No, mother—at least nothing that could possibly explain his givin' me up.

Mrs. Boyle. You know you're a bit hasty at times, Mary, an' say things you shouldn't say.

Mary. I never said to him what I shouldn't say, I'm sure of that.

Mrs. Boyle. How are you sure of it?

Mary. Because I love him with all my heart and soul, mother. Why, I don't know; I often thought to myself that he wasn't the man poor Jerry was, but I couldn't help loving him, all the same.

Mrs. Boyle. But you shouldn't be frettin' the way you

51

are; when a woman loses a man, she never knows what she's
afther losin', to be sure, but, then, she never knows what she's
afther gainin', either. You're not the one girl of a month ago
—you look like one pinin' away. It's long ago I had a right
to bring you to the doctor, instead of waitin' till to-night.

Mary. There's no necessity, really, mother, to go to the
doctor; nothing serious is wrong with me—I'm run down and
disappointed, that's all.

Mrs. Boyle. I'll not wait another minute; I don't like the
look of you at all. . . . I'm afraid we made a mistake in
throwin' over poor Jerry. . . . He'd have been betther for
you than that Bentham.

Mary. Mother, the best man for a woman is the one for
whom she has the most love, and Charlie had it all.

Mrs. Boyle. Well, there's one thing to be said for him—
he couldn't have been thinkin' of the money, or he wouldn't
ha' left you . . . it must ha' been somethin' else.

Mary (wearily). I don't know . . . I don't know, mother
. . . only I think . . .

Mrs. Boyle. What d'ye think?

Mary. I imagine . . . he thought . . . we weren't . . .
good enough for him.

Mrs. Boyle. An' what was he himself, only a school
teacher? Though I don't blame him for fightin' shy of
people like that Joxer fella an' that oul' Madigan wan—
nice sort o' people for your father to inthroduce to a man
like Mr. Bentham. You might have told me all about this
before now, Mary; I don't know why you like to hide everything from your mother; you knew Bentham, an' I'd ha' known
nothin' about it if it hadn't bin for the Will; an' it was only
to-day, afther long coaxin', that you let out that he's left you.

Mary. It would have been useless to tell you—you
wouldn't understand.

Mrs. Boyle (hurt). Maybe not. . . . Maybe I wouldn't
understand. . . . Well, we'll be off now.

[*She goes over to door left, and speaks to* Boyle *inside.*

Mrs. Boyle. We're goin' now to the doctor's. Are you goin' to get up this evenin'?

Boyle (from inside). The pains in me legs is terrible! It's me should be poppin' off to the doctor instead o' Mary, the way I feel.

Mrs. Boyle. Sorra mend you! A nice way you were in last night—carried in in a frog's march, dead to the world. If that's the way you'll go on when you get the money it'll be the grave for you, an asylum for me and the Poorhouse for Johnny.

Boyle. I thought you were goin'?

Mrs. Boyle. That's what has you as you are—you can't bear to be spoken to. Knowin' the way we are, up to our ears in debt, it's a wondher you wouldn't ha' got up to go to th' solicitor's an' see if we could ha' gotten a little o' the money even.

Boyle (shouting). I can't be goin' up there night, noon an' mornin', can I? He can't give the money till he gets it, can he? I can't get blood out of a turnip, can I?

Mrs. Boyle. It's nearly two months since we heard of the Will, an' the money seems as far off as ever. . . . I suppose you know we owe twenty pouns to oul' Murphy?

Boyle. I've a faint recollection of you tellin' me that before.

Mrs. Boyle. Well, you'll go over to the shop yourself for the things in future—I'll face him no more.

Boyle. I thought you said you were goin'?

Mrs. Boyle. I'm goin' now; come on, Mary.

Boyle. Ey, Juno, ey!

Mrs. Boyle. Well, what d'ye want now?

Boyle. Is there e'er a bottle o' stout left?

Mrs. Boyle. There's two o' them here still.

Boyle. Show us in one o' them an' leave t'other there till I get up. An' throw us in the paper that's on the table, an' the bottle o' Sloan's Liniment that's in th' drawer.

Mrs. Boyle (*getting the liniment and the stout*). What paper is it you want—the *Messenger*?

Boyle. Messenger! The *News o' the World*!

> [*Mrs. Boyle brings in the things asked for, and comes out again.*

Mrs. Boyle (*at door*). Mind the candle, now, an' don't burn the house over our heads. I left t'other bottle o' stout on the table.

> [*She puts bottle of stout on table. She goes out with* Mary. *A cork is heard popping inside.*

> [*A pause; then outside the door is heard the voice of* Joxer *lilting softly:* ' *Me pipe I'll smoke, as I dhrive me moke . . . are you . . . there . . . Mor . . . ee . . . ar . . . i . . . teee!*' *A gentle knock is heard, and after a pause the door opens, and* Joxer, *followed by* Nugent, *enters.*

Joxer. Be God, they must be all out; I was thinkin' there was somethin' up when he didn't answer the signal. We seen Juno an' Mary goin', but I didn't see him, an' it's very seldom he escapes me.

Nugent. He's not goin' to escape me—he's not goin' to be let go to the fair altogether.

Joxer. Sure, the house couldn't hould them lately; an' he goin' about like a mastherpiece of the Free State counthry; forgettin' their friends; forgettin' God—wouldn't even lift his hat passin' a chapel! Sure they were bound to get a dhrop! An' you really think there's no money comin' to him afther all?

Nugent. Not as much as a red rex, man; I've been a bit anxious this long time over me money, an' I went up to the solicitor's to find out all I could—ah, man, they were goin' to throw me down the stairs. They toul' me that the oul' cock himself had the stairs worn away comin' up afther it, an' they black in the face tellin' him he'd get nothin'. Some way or another that the Will is writ he won't be entitled to get as much as a make!

Joxer. Ah, I thought there was somethin' curious about the whole thing; I've bin havin' sthrange dhreams for the last couple o' weeks. An' I notice that that Bentham fella doesn't be comin' here now—there must be somethin' on the mat there too. Anyhow, who, in the name o' God, ud leave anythin' to that oul' bummer? Sure it ud be unnatural. An' the way Juno an' him's been throwin' their weight about for the last few months! Ah, him that goes a borrowin' goes a sorrowin'!

Nugent. Well, he's not goin' to throw his weight about in the suit I made for him much longer. I'm tellin' you seven pouns aren't to be found growin' on the bushes these days.

Joxer. An' there isn't hardly a neighbour in the whole street that hasn't lent him money on the strength of what he was goin' to get, but they're after backing the wrong horse. Wasn't it a mercy o' God that I'd nothin' to give him! The softy I am, you know, I'd ha' lent him me last juice! I must have had somebody's good prayers. Ah, afther all, an honest man's the noblest work o' God!

                        [Boyle *coughs inside.*

Joxer. Whisht, damn it, he must be inside in bed.

Nugent. Inside o' bed or outside of it, he's goin' to pay me for that suit, or give it back—he'll not climb up my back as easily as he thinks.

Joxer. Gwan in at wanst, man, an' get it off him, an' don't be a fool.

Nugent (*going to door left, opening it and looking in*). Ah, don't disturb yourself, Mr. Boyle; I hope you're not sick?

Boyle. Th' oul' legs, Mr. Nugent, the oul' legs.

Nugent. I just called over to see if you could let me have anything off the suit?

Boyle. E-e-e-eh, how much is this it is?

Nugent. It's the same as it was at the start—seven pouns.

Boyle. I'm glad you kem, Mr. Nugent; I want a good

heavy top-coat—Irish frieze, if you have it. How much would a top-coat like that be, now?

Nugent. About six pouns.

Boyle. Six pouns—six an' seven, six an' seven is thirteen—that'll be thirteen pouns I'll owe you.

> [Joxer *slips the bottle of stout that is on the table into his pocket.* Nugent *rushes into the room, and returns with suit on his arm; he pauses at the door.*

Nugent. You'll owe me no thirteen pouns. Maybe you think you're betther able to owe it than pay it!

Boyle (*frantically*). Here, come back to hell ower that—where're you goin' with them clothes o' mine?

Nugent. Where am I goin' with them clothes o' yours? Well, I like your damn cheek!

Boyle. Here, what am I goin' to dhress meself in when I'm goin' out?

Nugent. What do I care what you dhress yourself in! You can put yourself in a bolsther cover, if you like.

> [*He goes towards the other door, followed by* Joxer.

Joxer. What'll he dhress himself in! Gentleman Jack an' his frieze coat!   [*They go out.*

Boyle (*inside*). Ey, Nugent; ey, Mr. Nugent, Mr. Nugent!

> [*After a pause* Boyle *enters hastily, buttoning the braces of his moleskin trousers; his coat and vest are on his arm; he throws these on a chair and hurries to the door on right.*

Boyle. Ey, Mr. Nugent, Mr. Nugent!

Joxer (*meeting him at the door*). What's up, what's wrong, Captain?

Boyle. Nugent's been here an' took away me suit—the only things I had to go out in!

Joxer. Tuk your suit—for God's sake! An' what were you doin' while he was takin' them?

Boyle. I was in bed when he stole in like a thief in the night, an' before I knew even what he was thinkin' of, he whipped them from the chair an' was off like a redshank!

Joxer. An' what, in the name o' God, did he do that for?

Boyle. What did he do it for? How the hell do I know what he done it for?—jealousy an' spite, I suppose.

Joxer. Did he not say what he done it for?

Boyle. Amn't I afther tellin' you that he had them whipped up an' was gone before I could open me mouth?

Joxer. That was a very sudden thing to do; there mus' be somethin' behin' it. Did he hear anythin', I wondher?

Boyle. Did he hear anythin'?—you talk very queer, Joxer —what could he hear?

Joxer. About you not gettin' the money,. in some way or t'other?

Boyle. An' what ud prevent me from gettin' th' money?

Joxer. That's jus' what I was thinkin'—what ud prevent you from gettin' the money—nothin', as far as I can see.

Boyle (looking round for bottle of stout, with an exclamation). Aw, holy God!

Joxer. What's up, Jack?

Boyle. He must have afther lifted the bottle o' stout that Juno left on the table!

Joxer (horrified). Ah no, ah no; he wouldn't be afther doin' that now.

Boyle. An' who done it then? Juno left a bottle o' stout here, an' it's gone—it didn't walk, did it?

Joxer. Oh, that's shockin'; ah, man's inhumanity to man makes countless thousands mourn!

Mrs. Madigan (appearing at the door). I hope I'm not disturbin' you in any discussion on your forthcomin' legacy— if I may use the word—an' that you'll let me have a barny for a minute or two with you, Mr. Boyle.

Boyle (uneasily). To be sure, Mrs. Madigan—an oul' friend's always welcome.

Joxer. Come in the evenin', come in th' mornin'; come when you're assed, or come without warnin', Mrs. Madigan.

Boyle. Sit down, Mrs. Madigan.

Mrs. Madigan (ominously). Th' few words I have to say can be said standin'. Puttin' aside all formularies, I suppose you remember me lendin' you some time ago three pouns that I raised on blankets an' furniture in me uncle's?

Boyle. I remember it well. I have it recorded in me book—three pouns five shillings from Maisie Madigan, raised on articles pawned; an', item: fourpence, given to make up the price of a pint, on th' principle that no bird ever flew on wan wing; all to be repaid at par, when the ship comes home.

Mrs. Madigan. Well, ever since I shoved in the blankets I've been perishing with th' cowld, an' I've decided, if I'll be too hot in th' next' world aself, I'm not goin' to be too cowld in this wan; an' consequently, I want me three pouns, if you please.

Boyle. This is a very sudden demand, Mrs. Madigan, an' can't be met; but I'm willin' to give you a receipt in full, in full.

Mrs. Madigan. Come on, out with th' money, an' don't be jack-actin'.

Boyle. You can't get blood out of a turnip, can you?

Mrs. Madigan (rushing over and shaking him). Gimme me money, y'oul' reprobate, or I'll shake the worth of it out of you!

Boyle. Ey, houl' on, there; houl' on, there! You'll wait for your money now, me lassie!

Mrs. Madigan (looking around the room and seeing the gramophone). I'll wait for it, will I? Well, I'll not wait long; if I can't get th' cash, I'll get th' worth of it.

> [*She catches up the gramophone.*

Boyle. Ey, ey, there, wher'r you goin' with that?

Mrs. Madigan. I'm goin' to th' pawn to get me three quid five shillins; I'll brin' you th' ticket, an' then you can do what you like, me bucko.

Boyle. You can't touch that, you can't touch that! It's not my property, an' it's not ped for yet!

Mrs. Madigan. So much th' better. It'll be an ayse to me conscience, for I'm takin' what doesn't belong to you. You're not goin' to be swankin' it like a paycock with Maisie Madigan's money—I'll pull some o' th' gorgeous feathers out o' your tail!   [*She goes off with the gramophone.*

Boyle. What's th' world comin' to at all? I ass you, Joxer Daly, is there any morality left anywhere?

Joxer. I wouldn't ha' believed it, only I seen it with me own two eyes. I didn't think Maisie Madigan was that sort of woman; she has either a sup taken, or she's heard somethin'.

Boyle. Heard somethin'—about what, if it's not any harm to ass you?

Joxer. She must ha' heard some rumour or other that you weren't goin' to get th' money.

Boyle. Who says I'm not goin' to get th' money?

Joxer. Sure, I don't know—I was only sayin'.

Boyle. Only sayin' what?

Joxer. Nothin'.

Boyle. You were goin' to say somethin'—don't be a twisther.

Joxer (angrily). Who's a twisther?

Boyle. Why don't you speak your mind, then?

Joxer. You never twisted yourself—no, you wouldn't know how!

Boyle. Did you ever know me to twist; did you ever know me to twist?

Joxer (fiercely). Did you ever do anythin' else! Sure, you can't believe a word that comes out o' your mouth.

Boyle. Here, get out, ower o' this; I always knew you were a prognosticator an' a procrastinator!

Joxer (going out as Johnny *comes in).* The anchor's weighed, farewell, ree . . . mem . . . ber . . . me. Jacky Boyle, Esquire, infernal rogue an' damned liar.

Johnny. Joxer an' you at it agen?—when are you goin'

to have a little respect for yourself, an' not be always makin'
a show of us all?

Boyle.   Are you goin' to lecture me now?

Johnny.   Is mother back from the doctor yet, with Mary?

> [*Mrs. Boyle enters; it is apparent from the serious look on
> her face that something has happened. She takes off her
> hat and coat without a word and puts them by. She then
> sits down near the fire, and there is a few moments' pause.*

Boyle.   Well, what did the doctor say about Mary?

Mrs. Boyle (*in an earnest manner and with suppressed agitation*).
Sit down here, Jack; I've something to say to you . . . about
Mary.

Boyle (*awed by her manner*).   About . . . Mary?

Mrs. Boyle.   Close that door there and sit down here.

Boyle (*closing the door*).   More throuble in our native land,
is it?   (*He sits down.*)   Well, what is it?

Mrs. Boyle.   It's about Mary.

Boyle.   Well, what about Mary—there's nothin' wrong
with her, is there?

Mrs. Boyle.   I'm sorry to say there's a gradle wrong with her.

Boyle.   A gradle wrong with her!   (*Peevishly*) First Johnny
an' now Mary; is the whole house goin' to become an hospital!   It's not consumption, is it?

Mrs. Boyle.   No . . . it's not consumption . . . it's worse.

Johnny.   Worse!   Well, we'll have to get her into some
place ower this, there's no one here to mind her.

Mrs. Boyle.   We'll all have to mind her now.   You might
as well know now, Johnny, as another time.   (*To* Boyle)
D'ye know what the doctor said to me about her, Jack?

Boyle.   How ud I know—I wasn't there, was I?

Mrs. Boyle.   He told me to get her married at wanst.

Boyle.   Married at wanst!   An' why did he say the like
o' that?

Mrs. Boyle.   Because Mary's goin' to have a baby in a short
time.

Boyle. Goin' to have a baby!—my God, what'll Bentham say when he hears that?

Mrs. Boyle. Are you blind, man, that you can't see that it was Bentham that has done this wrong to her?

Boyle (passionately). Then he'll marry her, he'll have to marry her!

Mrs. Boyle. You know he's gone to England, an' God knows where he is now.

Boyle. I'll folly him, I'll folly him, an' bring him back, an' make him do her justice. The scoundrel, I might ha' known what he was, with his yogees an' his prawna!

Mrs. Boyle. We'll have to keep it quiet till we see what we can do.

Boyle. Oh, isn't this a nice thing to come on top o' me, an' the state I'm in! A pretty show I'll be to Joxer an' to that oul' wan, Madigan! Amn't I afther goin' through enough without havin' to go through this!

Mrs. Boyle. What you an' I'll have to go through'll be nothin' to what poor Mary'll have to go through; for you an' me is middlin' old, an' most of our years is spent; but Mary'll have maybe forty years to face an' handle, an' every wan of them'll be tainted with a bitther memory.

Boyle. Where is she? Where is she till I tell her off? I'm tellin' you when I'm done with her she'll be a sorry girl!

Mrs. Boyle. I left her in me sister's till I came to speak to you. You'll say nothin' to her, Jack; ever since she left school she's earned her livin', an' your fatherly care never throubled the poor girl.

Boyle. Gwan, take her part agen her father! But I'll let you see whether I'll say nothin' to her or no! Her an' her readin'! That's more o' th' blasted nonsense that has the house fallin' down on top of us! What did th' likes of her, born in a tenement house, want with readin'? Her readin's afther bringin' her to a nice pass—oh, it's madnin', madnin', madnin'!

Mrs. Boyle. When she comes back say nothin' to her, Jack, or she'll leave this place.

Boyle. Leave this place! Ay, she'll leave this place, an' quick too!

Mrs. Boyle. If Mary goes, I'll go with her.

Boyle. Well, go with her! Well, go, th' pair o' yous! I lived before I seen yous, an' I can live when yous are gone. Isn't this a nice thing to come rollin' in on top o' me afther all your prayin' to St. Anthony an' The Little Flower! An' she's a Child o' Mary, too—I wonder what'll the nuns think of her now? An' it'll be bellows'd all over th' disthrict before you could say Jack Robinson; an' whenever I'm seen they'll whisper, 'That's th' father of Mary Boyle that had th' kid be th' swank she used to go with; d'ye know, d'ye know?' To be sure they'll know—more about it than I will meself!

Johnny. She should be dhriven out o' th' house she's brought disgrace on!

Mrs. Boyle. Hush, you, Johnny. We needn't let it be bellows'd all over the place; all we've got to do is to leave this place quietly an' go somewhere where we're not known an' nobody'll be th' wiser.

Boyle. You're talkin' like a two-year-oul', woman. Where'll we get a place ou' o' this?—places aren't that easily got.

Mrs. Boyle. But, Jack, when we get the money . . .

Boyle. Money—what money?

Mrs. Boyle. Why, oul' Ellison's money, of course.

Boyle. There's no money comin' from oul' Ellison, or any one else. Since you've heard of wan throuble, you might as well hear of another. There's no money comin' to us at all—the Will's a wash-out!

Mrs. Boyle. What are you sayin', man—no money?

Johnny. How could it be a wash-out?

Boyle. The boyo that's afther doin' it to Mary done it to me as well. The thick made out the Will wrong; he said in

th' Will, only first cousin an' second cousin, instead of
mentionin' our names, an' now any one that thinks he's a first
cousin or second 'cousin t'oul' Ellison can claim the money as
well as me, an' they're springin' up in hundreds, an' comin'
from America an' Australia, thinkin' to get their whack out of
it, while all the time the lawyers is gobblin' it up, till there's
not as much as ud buy a stockin' for your lovely daughter's
baby!

Mrs. Boyle. I don't believe it, I don't believe it, I don't
believe it!

Johnny. Why did you say nothin' about this before?

Mrs. Boyle. You're not serious, Jack; you're not serious!

Boyle. I'm tellin' you the scholar, Bentham, made a
banjax o' th' Will; instead o' sayin', 'th' rest o' me property
to be divided between me first cousin, Jack Boyle, an' me
second cousin, Mick Finnegan, o' Santhry', he writ down only,
'me first an' second cousins', an' the world an' his wife are
afther th' property now.

Mrs. Boyle. Now I know why Bentham left poor Mary
in th' lurch; I can see it all now—oh, is there not even a
middlin' honest man left in th' world?

Johnny (*to* Boyle). An' you let us run into debt, an' you
borreyed money from everybody to fill yourself with beer!
An' now you tell us the whole thing's a washout! Oh, if it's
thrue, I'm done with you, for you're worse than me sisther
Mary!

Boyle. You hole your tongue, d'ye hear? I'll not take
any lip from you. Go an' get Bentham if you want satisfaction for all that's afther happenin' us.

Johnny. I won't hole me tongue, I won't hole me tongue!
I'll tell you what I think of you, father an' all as you are . . .
you . . .

Mrs. Boyle. Johnny, Johnny, Johnny, for God's sake, be
quiet!

Johnny. I'll not be quiet, I'll not be quiet; he's a nice

father, isn't he? Is it any wondher Mary went asthray,
when . . .

Mrs. Boyle. Johnny, Johnny, for my sake be quiet—for
your mother's sake!

Boyle. I'm goin' out now to have a few dhrinks with th'
last few makes I have, an' tell that lassie o' yours not to be here
when I come back; for if I lay me eyes on her, I'll lay me hans
on her, an' if I lay me hans on her, I won't be accountable for
me actions!

Johnny. Take care somebody doesn't lay his hans on you
—y'oul' . . .

Mrs. Boyle. Johnny, Johnny!

Boyle (*at door, about to go out*). Oh, a nice son, an' a nicer
daughter, I have. (*Calling loudly upstairs*) Joxer, Joxer, are
you there?

Joxer (*from a distance*). I'm here, More . . . ee . . . aar
. . . i . . . tee!

Boyle. I'm goin' down to Foley's—are you comin'?

Joxer. Come with you? With that sweet call me heart
is stirred; I'm only waiting for the word, an' I'll be with you,
like a bird!   [*Boyle and* Joxer *pass the door going out.*

Johnny (*throwing himself on the bed*). I've a nice sisther, an'
a nice father, there's no bettin' on it. I wish to God a
bullet or a bomb had whipped me ou' o' this long ago!
Not one o' yous, not one o' yous, have any thought for
me!

Mrs. Boyle (*with passionate remonstrance*). If you don't
whisht, Johnny, you'll drive me mad. Who has kep' th'
home together for the past few years—only me? An' who'll
have to bear th' biggest part o' this throuble but me?—but
whinin' an' whingin' isn't goin' to do any good.

Johnny. You're to blame yourself for a gradle of it—givin'
him his own way in everything, an' never assin' to check him,
no matther what he done. Why didn't you look afther th'
money? why . . .

[*There is a knock at the door; Mrs. Boyle opens it; Johnny rises on his elbow to look and listen; two men enter.*

First Man. We've been sent up be th' Manager of the Hibernian Furnishing Co., Mrs. Boyle, to take back the furniture that was got a while ago.

Mrs. Boyle. Yous'll touch nothin' here—how do I know who yous are?

First Man (*showing a paper*). There's the ordher, ma'am. (*Reading*) A chest o' drawers, a table, wan easy an' two ordinary chairs; wan mirror; wan chesterfield divan, an' a wardrobe an' two vases. (*To his comrade*) Come on, Bill, it's afther knockin'-off time already.

Johnny. For God's sake, mother, run down to Foley's an' bring father back, or we'll be left without a stick.

[*The men carry out the tables.*

Mrs. Boyle. What good would it be?—you heard what he said before he went out.

Johnny. Can't you thry? He ought to be here, an' the like of this goin' on.

[*Mrs. Boyle puts a shawl around her, as Mary enters.*

Mary. What's up, mother? I met men carryin' away the table, an' everybody's talking about us not gettin' the money after all.

Mrs. Boyle. Everythin's gone wrong, Mary, everythin'. We're not gettin' a penny out o' the Will, not a penny—I'll tell you all when I come back; I'm goin' for your father.

[*She runs out.*

Johnny (*to Mary, who has sat down by the fire*). It's a wondher you're not ashamed to show your face here, afther what has happened.

[*Jerry enters slowly; there is a look of earnest hope on his face. He looks at Mary for a few moments.*

Jerry (*softly*). Mary!   [*Mary does not answer.*

Jerry. Mary, I want to speak to you for a few moments, may I?

[*Mary remains silent;* Johnny *goes slowly into room on left.*

Jerry. Your mother has told me everything, Mary, and I have come to you. . . . I have come to tell you, Mary, that my love for you is greater and deeper than ever. . . .

Mary (*with a sob*). Oh, Jerry, Jerry, say no more; all that is over now; anything like that is impossible now!

Jerry. Impossible? Why do you talk like that, Mary?

Mary. After all that has happened.

Jerry. What does it matter what has happened? We are young enough to be able to forget all those things. (*He catches her hand*) Mary, Mary, I am pleading for your love. With Labour, Mary, humanity is above everything; we are the Leaders in the fight for a new life. I want to forget Bentham, I want to forget that you left me—even for a while.

Mary. Oh, Jerry, Jerry, you haven't the bitter word of scorn for me after all.

Jerry (*passionately*). Scorn! I love you, love you, Mary!

Mary (*rising, and looking him in the eyes*). Even though . . .

Jerry. Even though you threw me over for another man; even though you gave me many a bitter word!

Mary. Yes, yes, I know; but you love me, even though . . . even though . . . I'm . . . goin' . . . goin' . . . (*He looks at her questioningly, and fear gathers in his eyes.*) Ah, I was thinkin' so. . . . You don't know everything!

Jerry (*poignantly*). Surely to God, Mary, you don't mean that . . . that . . . that . . .

Mary. Now you know all, Jerry; now you know all!

Jerry. My God, Mary, have you fallen as low as that?

Mary. Yes, Jerry, as you say, I have fallen as low as that.

Jerry. I didn't mean it that way, Mary . . . it came on me so sudden, that I didn't mind what I was sayin'. . . . I never expected this—your mother never told me. . . . I'm sorry . . . God knows, I'm sorry for you, Mary.

Mary. Let us say no more, Jerry; I don't blame you for

thinkin' it's terrible. . . . I suppose it is. . . . Everybody'll think the same . . . it's only as I expected—your humanity is just as narrow as the humanity of the others.

Jerry. I'm sorry, all the same. . . . I shouldn't have troubled you. . . . I wouldn't if I'd known. . . . If I can do anything for you . . . Mary . . . I will.

> [*He turns to go, and halts at the door.*

Mary. Do you remember, Jerry, the verses you read when you gave the lecture in the Socialist Rooms some time ago, on Humanity's Strife with Nature?

Jerry. The verses—no; I don't remember them.

Mary. I do. They're runnin' in me head now—

> An' we felt the power that fashion'd
> All the lovely things we saw,
> That created all the murmur
> Of an everlasting law,
> Was a hand of force an' beauty,
> With an eagle's tearin' claw.

> Then we saw our globe of beauty
> Was an ugly thing as well,
> A hymn divine whose chorus
> Was an agonizin' yell;
> Like the story of a demon,
> That an angel had to tell;

> Like a glowin' picture by a
> Hand unsteady, brought to ruin;
> Like her craters, if their deadness
> Could give life unto the moon;
> Like the agonizing horror
> Of a violin out of tune.

> [*There is a pause, and* Devine *goes slowly out.*

Johnny (returning). Is he gone?

Mary. Yes.

> [*The two men re-enter.*

First Man. We can't wait any longer for t'oul' fella—sorry, Miss, but we have to live as well as th' nex' man.

> [*They carry out some things.*

Johnny. Oh, isn't this terrible! . . . I suppose you told him everything . . . couldn't you have waited for a few days? . . . he'd have stopped th' takin' of the things, if you'd kep' your mouth shut. Are you burnin' to tell every one of the shame you've brought on us?

Mary (*snatching up her hat and coat*). Oh, this is unbearable!

> [*She rushes out.*

First Man (*re-entering*). We'll take the chest o' drawers next—it's the heaviest.

> [*The votive light flickers for a moment, and goes out.*

Johnny (*in a cry of fear*). Mother o' God, the light's afther goin' out!

First Man. You put the win' up me the way you bawled that time. The oil's all gone, that's all.

Johnny (*with an agonizing cry*). Mother o' God, there's a shot I'm afther gettin'!

First Man. What's wrong with you, man? Is it a fit you're takin'?

Johnny. I'm afther feelin' a pain in me breast, like the tearin' by of a bullet!

First Man. He's goin' mad—it's a wondher they'd leave a chap like that here by himself.

> [*Two Irregulars enter swiftly; they carry revolvers; one goes over to* Johnny; *the other covers the two furniture men.*

First Irregular (*to the men, quietly and incisively*). Who are you?—what are yous doin' here?—quick!

First Man. Removin' furniture that's not paid for.

Irregular. Get over to the other end of the room an' turn your faces to the wall—quick!

> [*The two men turn their faces to the wall, with their hands up.*

Second Irregular (*to* Johnny). Come on, Sean Boyle, you're wanted; some of us have a word to say to you.

Johnny. I'm sick, I can't—what do you want with me?

Second Irregular. Come on, come on; we've a distance to go, an' haven't much time—come on.

Johnny. I'm an oul' comrade—yous wouldn't shoot an oul' comrade.

Second Irregular. Poor Tancred was an oul' comrade o' yours, but you didn't think o' that when you gave him away to the gang that sent him to his grave. But we've no time to waste; come on—here, Dermot, ketch his arm. (*To* Johnny) Have you your beads?

Johnny. Me beads! Why do you ass me that, why do you ass me that?

Second Irregular. Go on, go on, march!

Johnny. Are yous goin' to do in a comrade?—look at me arm, I lost it for Ireland.

Second Irregular. Commandant Tancred lost his life for Ireland.

Johnny. Sacred Heart of Jesus, have mercy on me! Mother o' God, pray for me—be with me now in the agonies o' death! . . . Hail, Mary, full o' grace . . . the Lord is . . . with Thee.

> [*They drag out* Johnny Boyle, *and the curtain falls. When it rises again the most of the furniture is gone.* Mary *and* Mrs. Boyle, *one on each side, are sitting in a darkened room, by the fire; it is an hour later.*

Mrs. Boyle. I'll not wait much longer . . . what did they bring him away in the mothor for? Nugent says he thinks they had guns . . . is me throubles never goin' to be over? . . . If anything ud happen to poor Johnny, I think I'd lose me mind. . . . I'll go to the Police Station, surely they ought to be able to do somethin'.

> [*Below is heard the sound of voices.*

Mrs. Boyle. Whisht, is that something? Maybe, it's

your father, though when I left him in Foley's he was hardly able to lift his head.　Whisht!

　　　　[*A knock at the door, and the voice of* Mrs. Madigan, *speaking very softly*]: Mrs. Boyle, Mrs. Boyle.

　　　　　　　　　　　　　　　　[Mrs. Boyle *opens the door.*

Mrs. Madigan.　Oh, Mrs. Boyle, God an' His Blessed Mother be with you this night!

Mrs. Boyle (*calmly*).　What is it, Mrs. Madigan?　It's Johnny—something about Johnny.

Mrs. Madigan.　God send it's not, God send it's not Johnny!

Mrs. Boyle.　Don't keep me waitin', Mrs. Madigan; I've gone through so much lately that I feel able for anything.

Mrs. Madigan.　Two polismen below wantin' you.

Mrs. Boyle.　Wantin' me; an' why do they want me?

Mrs. Madigan.　Some poor fella's been found, an' they think it's, it's . . .

Mrs. Boyle.　Johnny, Johnny!

Mary (*with her arms round her mother*).　Oh, mother, mother, me poor, darlin' mother.

Mrs. Boyle. . Hush, hush, darlin'; you'll shortly have your own throuble to bear.　(*To* Mrs. Madigan) An' why do the polis think it's Johnny, Mrs. Madigan?

Mrs. Madigan.　Because one o' the doctors knew him when he was attendin' with his poor arm.

Mrs. Boyle.　Oh, it's thrue, then; it's Johnny, it's me son, me own son!

Mary.　Oh, it's thrue, it's thrue what Jerry Devine says—there isn't a God, there isn't a God; if there was He wouldn't let these things happen!

Mrs. Boyle.　Mary, you mustn't say them things.　We'll want all the help we can get from God an' His Blessed Mother now!　These things have nothin' to do with the Will o' God. Ah, what can God do agen the stupidity o' men!

Mrs. Madigan. The polis want you to go with them to the hospital to see the poor body—they're waitin' below.

Mrs. Boyle. We'll go. Come, Mary, an' we'll never come back here agen. Let your father furrage for himself now; I've done all I could an' it was all no use—he'll be hopeless till the end of his days. I've got a little room in me sisther's where we'll stop till your throuble is over, an' then we'll work together for the sake of the baby.

Mary. My poor little child that'll have no father!

Mrs. Boyle. It'll have what's far betther—it'll have two mothers.

A Rough Voice shouting from below. Are yous goin' to keep us waitin' for yous all night?

Mrs. Madigan (going to the door, and shouting down). Take your hour, there, take your hour! If yous are in such a hurry, skip off, then, for nobody wants you here—if they did yous wouldn't be found. For you're the same as yous were undher the British Government—never where yous are wanted! As far as I can see, the Polis as Polis, in this city, is Null an' Void!

Mrs. Boyle. We'll go, Mary, we'll go; you to see your poor dead brother, an' me to see me poor dead son!

Mary. I dhread it, mother, I dhread it!

Mrs. Boyle. I forgot, Mary, I forgot; your poor oul' selfish mother was only thinkin' of herself. No, no, you mustn't come—it wouldn't be good for you. You go on to me sisther's an' I'll face th' ordeal meself. Maybe I didn't feel sorry enough for Mrs. Tancred when her poor son was found as Johnny's been found now—because he was a Diehard! Ah, why didn't I remember that then he wasn't a Diehard or a Stater, but only a poor dead son! It's well I remember all that she said—an' it's my turn to say it now: What was the pain I suffered, Johnny, bringin' you into the world to carry you to your cradle, to the pains I'll suffer carryin' you out o' the world to bring you to your grave! Mother o' God, Mother o' God, have pity on us all! Blessed

Virgin, where were you when me darlin' son was riddled with bullets, when me darlin' son was riddled with bullets? Sacred Heart o' Jesus, take away our hearts o' stone, and give us hearts o' flesh! Take away this murdherin' hate, an' give us Thine own eternal love!   [*They all go slowly out.*

> [*There is a pause; then a sound of shuffling steps on the stairs outside. The door opens and* Boyle *and* Joxer, *both of them very drunk, enter.*

Boyle. I'm able to go no farther. . . . Two polis, ey . . . what were they doin' here, I wondher? . . . Up to no good, anyhow . . . an' Juno an' that lovely daughter o' mine with them. (*Taking a sixpence from his pocket and looking at it*) Wan single, solitary tanner left out of all I borreyed . . . . (*He lets it fall.*) The last o' the Mohicans. . . . The blinds is down, Joxer, the blinds is down!

Joxer (*walking unsteadily across the room, and anchoring at the bed*). Put all . . . your throubles . . . in your oul' kit-bag . . . an' smile . . . smile . . . smile!

Boyle. The counthry'll have to steady itself . . . it's goin' . . . to hell. . . . Where'r all . . . the chairs . . . gone to . . . steady itself, Joxer. . . . Chairs'll . . . have to . . . steady themselves. . . . No matther . . . what any one may . . . say. . . . Irelan' sober . . . is Irelan' . . . free.

Joxer (*stretching kimself on the bed*). Chains . . . an' . . . slaveree . . . that's a darlin' motto . . . a daaarlin' . . . motto!

Boyle. If th' worst comes . . . to th' worse . . . I can join a . . . flyin' . . . column. . . . I done . . . me bit . . . in Easther Week . . . had no business . . . to . . . be . . . there . . . but Captain Boyle's Captain Boyle!

Joxer. Breathes there a man with soul . . . so . . . de . . . ad . . . this . . . me . . . o . . . wn, me nat . . . ive l . . . an'!

Boyle (*subsiding into a sitting posture on the floor*). Commandant Kelly died . . . in them . . . arms . . . Joxer. . . . Tell me Volunteer Butties . . . says he . . . that . . . I died for . . . Irelan'!

Joxer. D'jever rade Willie . . . Reilly . . . an' his own . . . Colleen . . . Bawn? It's a darlin' story, a daarlin' story!

Boyle. I'm telling you . . . Joxer . . . th' whole worl's . . . in a terr . . . ible state o' . . . chassis!

CURTAIN

THE SHADOW OF A GUNMAN
A Tragedy in Two Acts

CHARACTERS IN THE PLAY

Donal Davoren
Seumas Shields, *a pedlar*
Tommy Owens
Adolphus Grigson
Mrs. Grigson
Minnie Powell
} *Residents in the Tenement*

Mr. Mulligan, *the landlord*
Mr. Maguire, *soldier of the I.R.A.*
Mrs. Henderson
Mr. Gallogher
} *Residents of an adjoining Tenement*

An Auxiliary

SCENE

A room in a tenement in Hilljoy Square, Dublin.
Some hours elapse between the two acts. The period of
the Play is May 1920.

ACT I

A Return Room in a tenement house in Hilljoy Square. At the back two large windows looking out into the yard; they occupy practically the whole of the back wall space. Between the windows is a cupboard, on the top of which is a pile of books. The doors are open, and on these are hanging a number of collars and ties. Running parallel with the windows is a stretcher bed; another runs at right angles along the wall at right. At the head of this bed is a door leading to the rest of the house. The wall on the left runs diagonally, so that the fireplace—which is in the centre —is plainly visible. On the mantelshelf to the right is a statue of the Virgin, to the left a statue of the Sacred Heart, and in the centre a crucifix. Around the fireplace are a few common cooking utensils. In the centre of the room is a table, on which are a typewriter, a candle and candlestick, a bunch of wild flowers in a vase, writing materials and a number of books. There are two chairs, one near the fireplace and one at the table. The aspect of the place is one of absolute untidiness, engendered on the one hand by the congenital slovenliness of Seumas Shields, and on the other by the temperament of Donal Davoren, making it appear impossible to effect an improvement in such a place.

Davoren is sitting at the table typing. He is about thirty. There is in his face an expression that seems to indicate an eternal war between weakness and strength; there is in the lines of the brow and chin an indication of a desire for activity, while in his eyes there is visible an unquenchable tendency towards rest. His struggle through life has been a hard one, and his efforts have been handicapped by an inherited and self-developed devotion to 'the might of design, the mystery of colour, and the belief in the redemption of all things by beauty everlasting'. His life would drive him mad were it not for the fact that he never knew any other. He bears upon his body the marks of the struggle for existence and the efforts towards self-expression.

Seumas Shields, *who is in the bed next the wall to the right, is a heavily built man of thirty-five; he is dark-haired and sallow-complexioned. In him is frequently manifested the superstition, the fear and the malignity of primitive man.*

Davoren (*lilting an air as he composes*):

Or when sweet Summer's ardent arms outspread,
Entwined with flowers,
Enfold us, like two lovers newly wed,
Thro' ravish'd hours—
Then sorrow, woe and pain lose all their powers,
For each is dead, and life is only ours.

[*A woman's figure appears at the window and taps loudly on one of the panes; at the same moment there is loud knocking at the door.*

Voice of Woman at Window. Are you awake, Mr. Shields —Mr. Shields, are you awake? Are you goin' to get up to-day at all, at all?

Voice at the Door. Mr. Shields, is there any use of callin' you at all? This is a nice nine o'clock: do you know what time it is, Mr. Shields?

Seumas (*loudly*). Yes!

Voice at the Door. Why don't you get up, then, an' not have the house turned into a bedlam tryin' to waken you?

Seumas (*shouting*). All right, all right, all right! The way these oul' ones bawl at a body! Upon my soul! I'm beginnin' to believe that the Irish People are still in the stone age. If they could they'd throw a bomb at you.

Davoren. A land mine exploding under the bed is the only thing that would lift you out of it.

Seumas (*stretching himself*). Oh-h-h. I was fast in the arms of Morpheus—he was one of the infernal deities, son of Somnus, wasn't he?

Davoren. I think so.

Seumas. The poppy was his emblem, wasn't it?

Davoren. Ah, I don't know.

Seumas. It's a bit cold this morning, I think, isn't it?

Davoren. It's quite plain I'm not going to get much quietness in this house.

Seumas (after a pause). I wonder what time it is?

Davoren. The Angelus went some time ago.

Seumas (sitting up in bed suddenly). The Angelus! It couldn't be that late, could it? I asked them to call me at nine so that I could get Mass before I went on my rounds. Why didn't you give us a rap?

Davoren. Give you a rap! Why, man, they've been thundering at the door and hammering at the window for the past two hours, till the house shook to its very foundations, but you took less notice of the infernal din than I would take of the strumming of a grasshopper.

Seumas. There's no fear of you thinking of any one else when you're at your poetry. The land of Saints and Scholars 'ill shortly be a land of bloody poets. *(Anxiously)* I suppose Maguire has come and gone?

Davoren. Maguire? No, he hasn't been here—why, did you expect him?

Seumas (in a burst of indignation). He said he'd be here at nine. 'Before the last chime has struck,' says he, 'I'll be coming in on the door,' and it must be—what time is it now?

Davoren. Oh, it must be half-past twelve.

Seumas. Did anybody ever see the like of the Irish People? Is there any use of tryin' to do anything in this country? Have everything packed and ready, have everything packed and ready, have . . .

Davoren. And have you everything packed and ready?

Seumas. What's the use of having anything packed and ready when he didn't come? *(He rises and dresses himself.)* No wonder this unfortunate country is as it is, for you can't depend upon the word of a single individual in it. I suppose he was too damn lazy to get up; he wanted the streets to be well aired first.—Oh, Kathleen ni Houlihan, your way's a thorny way.

Davoren. Ah me! alas, pain, pain ever, for ever!

Seumas. That's from Shelley's *Prometheus Unbound.* I could never agree with Shelley, not that there's anything to be said against him as a poet—as a poet—but . . .

Davoren. He flung a few stones through stained-glass windows.

Seumas. He wasn't the first nor he won't be the last to do that, but the stained-glass windows—more than ever of them —are here still, and Shelley is doing a jazz dance down below.
[*He gives a snarling laugh of pleasure.*

Davoren (shocked). And you actually rejoice and are exceedingly glad that, as you believe, Shelley, the sensitive, high-minded, noble-hearted Shelley, is suffering the tortures of the damned.

Seumas. I rejoice in the vindication of the Church and Truth.

Davoren. Bah. You know as little about truth as anybody else, and you care as little about the Church as the least of those that profess her faith; your religion is simply the state of being afraid that God will torture your soul in the next world as you are afraid the Black and Tans will torture your body in this.

Seumas. Go on, me boy; I'll have a right laugh at you when both of us are dead.

Davoren. You're welcome to laugh as much as you like at me when both of us are dead.

Seumas (as he is about to put on his collar and tie). I don't think I need to wash meself this morning; do I look all right?

Davoren. Oh, you're all right; it's too late now to start washing yourself. Didn't you wash yourself yesterday morning?

Seumas. I gave meself a great rub yesterday. (*He pro-*

ceeds to pack various articles into an attaché case—spoons, forks, laces, thread, etc.) I think I'll bring out a few of the braces too; damn it, they're well worth sixpence each; there's great stuff in them—did you see them?

Davoren. Yes, you showed them to me before.

Seumas. They're great value; I only hope I'll be able to get enough o' them. I'm wearing a pair of them meself— they'd do Cuchullian, they're so strong. (*Counting the spoons*) There's a dozen in each of these parcels—three, six, nine— damn it, there's only eleven in this one. I better try another Three, six, nine—my God, there's only eleven in this one too, and one of them bent! Now I suppose I'll have to go through the whole bloody lot of them, for I'd never be easy in me mind thinkin' there'd be more than a dozen in some o' them. And still we're looking for freedom—ye gods, it's a glorious country! (*He lets one fall, which he stoops to pick up.*) Oh, my God, there's the braces after breakin'.

Davoren. That doesn't look as if they were strong enough for Cuchullian.

Seumas. I put a heavy strain on them too sudden. There's that fellow Maguire never turned up, either; he's almost too lazy to wash himself. (*As he is struggling with the braces the door is hastily shoved in and Maguire rushes in with a handbag.*) This is a nice nine o'clock. What's the use of you coming at this hour o' the day? Do you think we're going to work be moonlight? If you weren't goin' to come at nine couldn't you say you weren't. . . .

Maguire. Keep your hair on; I just blew in to tell you that I couldn't go to-day at all. I have to go to Knocksedan.

Seumas. Knocksedan! An' what, in the name o' God, is bringin' you to Knocksedan?

Maguire. Business, business. I'm going out to catch butterflies.

Seumas. If you want to make a cod of anybody, make a cod of somebody else, an' don't be tryin' to make a cod o' me.

Here I've had everything packed an' ready for hours; you were to be here at nine, an' you wait till just one o'clock to come rushin' in like a mad bull to say you've got to go to Knocksedan! Can't you leave Knocksedan till to-morrow?

Maguire. Can't be did, can't be did, Seumas; if I waited till to-morrow all the butterflies might be dead. I'll leave this bag here till this evening. (*He puts the bag in a corner of the room.*) Good-bye . . . ee.

> [*He is gone before Seumas is aware of it.*

Seumas (*with a gesture of despair*). Oh, this is a hopeless country! There's a fellow that thinks that the four cardinal virtues are not to be found outside an Irish Republic. I don't want to boast about myself—I don't want to boast about myself, and I suppose I could call meself as good a Gael as some of those that are knocking about now—knocking about now—as good a Gael as some that are knocking about now,—but I remember the time when I taught Irish six nights a week, when in the Irish Republican Brotherhood I paid me rifle levy like a man, an' when the Church refused to have anything to do with James Stephens, I tarred a prayer for the repose of his soul on the steps of the Pro-Cathedral. Now, after all me work for Dark Rosaleen, the only answer you can get from a roarin' Republican to a simple question is 'good-bye . . . ee'. What, in the name o' God, can be bringin' him to Knocksedan?

Davoren. Hadn't you better run out and ask him?

Seumas. That's right, that's right—make a joke about it! That's the Irish People all over—they treat a joke as a serious thing and a serious thing as a joke. Upon me soul, I'm beginning to believe that the Irish People aren't, never were, an' never will be fit for self-government. They made Balor of the Evil Eye King of Ireland, an' so signs on it there's neither conscience nor honesty from one end of the country to the other. Well, I hope he'll have a happy day in Knocksedan. (*A knock at the door.*) Who's that?   [*Another knock.*

Seumas (irritably). Who's that; who's there?

Davoren (more irritably). Halt and give the countersign—damn it, man, can't you go and see?

> [Seumas *goes over and opens the door. A man of about sixty is revealed, dressed in a faded blue serge suit; a half tall hat is on his head. It is evident that he has no love for Seumas, who denies him the deference he believes is due from a tenant to a landlord. He carries some papers in his hand.*

The Landlord (ironically). Good-day, Mr. Shields; it's meself that hopes you're feelin' well—you're lookin' well, anyhow—though you can't always go be looks nowadays.

Seumas. It doesn't matter whether I'm lookin' well or feelin' well; I'm all right, thanks be to God.

The Landlord. I'm very glad to hear it.

Seumas. It doesn't matter whether you're glad to hear it or not, Mr. Mulligan.

The Landlord. You're not inclined to be very civil, Mr. Shields.

Seumas. Look here, Mr. Mulligan, if you come here to raise an argument, I've something to do—let me tell you that.

The Landlord. I don't come here to raise no argument; a person ud have small gains argufyin' with you—let me tell you that.

Seumas. I've no time to be standin' here gostherin' with you—let me shut the door, Mr. Mulligan.

The Landlord. You'll not shut no door till you've heard what I've got to say.

Seumas. Well, say it then, an' go about your business.

The Landlord. You're very high an' mighty, but take care you're not goin' to get a drop. What a baby you are not to know what brings me here! Maybe you thought I was goin' to ask you to come to tea.

Davoren. Ah me! alas, pain, pain ever, for ever!

Seumas. Are you goin' to let me shut the door, Mr. Mulligan?

The Landlord. I'm here for me rent; you don't like the idea of bein' asked to pay your just an' lawful debts.

Seumas. You'll get your rent when you learn to keep your rent-book in a proper way.

The Landlord. I'm not goin' to take any lessons from you, anyhow.

Seumas. I want to have no more talk with you, Mr. Mulligan.

The Landlord. Talk or no talk, you owe me eleven weeks' rent, an' it's marked down again' you in black an' white.

Seumas. I don't care a damn if it was marked down in green, white, an' yellow.

The Landlord. You're a terribly independent fellow, an' it ud be fitter for you to be less funny an' stop tryin' to be billickin' honest an' respectable people.

Seumas. Just you be careful what you're sayin', Mr. Mulligan. There's law in the land still.

The Landlord. Be me sowl there is, an' you're goin' to get a little of it now. (*He offers the papers to* Seumas) Them's for you.

Seumas (*hesitating to take them*). I want to have nothing to do with you, Mr. Mulligan.

The Landlord (*throwing the papers in the centre of the room*). What am I better? It was the sorry day I ever let you come into this house. Maybe them notices to quit will stop your writin' letters to the papers about me an' me house.

Davoren. For goodness' sake, bring the man in, and don't be discussing the situation like a pair of primitive troglodytes.

Seumas (*taking no notice*). Writing letters to the papers is my business, an' I'll write as often as I like, when I like, an' how I like.

The Landlord. You'll not write about this house at all events. You can blow about the state of the yard, but you took care to say nothin' about payin' rent: oh no, that's not in your line. But since you're not satisfied with the house, you can pack up an' go to another.

Seumas.   I'll go, Mr. Mulligan, when I think fit, an' no sooner.

The Landlord.   Not content with keeping the rent, you're startin' to bring in lodgers—(*to* Davoren) not that I'm sayin' anythin' again' you, sir.   Bringin' in lodgers without as much as be your leave—what's the world comin' to at all that a man's house isn't his own?   But I'll soon put a stop to your gallop, for on the twenty-eight of the next month out you go, an' there'll be few sorry to see your back.

Seumas.   I'll go when I like.

The Landlord.   I'll let you see whether you own the house or no.

Seumas.   I'll go when I like!

The Landlord.   We'll see about that.

Seumas.   We'll see.

The Landlord.   Ay, we'll see.

[*The Landlord* goes out and Seumas *shuts the door.*

The Landlord (*outside*).   Mind you, I'm in earnest; you'll not stop in this house a minute longer than the twenty-eight.

Seumas (*with a roar*).   Ah, go to hell!

Davoren (*pacing the room as far as the space will permit*).   What in the name of God persuaded me to come to such a house as this?

Seumas.   It's nothing when you're used to it; you're too thin-skinned altogether.   The oul' sod's got the wind up about you, that's all.

Davoren.   Got the wind up about me!

Seumas.   He thinks you're on the run.   He's afraid of a raid, and that his lovely property'll be destroyed.

Davoren.   But why, in the name of all that's sensible, should he think that I'm on the run?

Seumas.   Sure they all think you're on the run.   Mrs. Henderson thinks it, Tommy Owens thinks it, Mrs. an' Mr. Grigson thinks it, an' Minnie Powell thinks it too.   (*Picking *up his attaché case*) I'd better be off if I'm goin' to do anything to-day.

Davoren. What are we going to do with these notices to quit?

Seumas. Oh, shove them up on the mantelpiece behind one of the statues.

Davoren. Oh, I mean what action shall we take?

Seumas. I haven't time to stop now. We'll talk about them when I come back. . . . I'll get me own back on that oul' Mulligan yet. I wish to God they would come an' smash his rookery to pieces, for it's all he thinks of, and, mind you, oul' Mulligan would call himself a descendant of the true Gaels of Banba—(*as he goes out*):

> Oh, proud were the chieftains of famed Inisfail.
> Is truagh gan oidher 'na Vfarradh.
> The stars of our sky an' the salt of our soil—

Oh, Kathleen ni Houlihan, your way's a thorny way!

> [*He goes out.*

Davoren (*returning to the table and sitting down at the type-writer*). Oh, Donal Og O'Davoren, your way's a thorny way. Your last state is worse than your first. Ah me, alas! Pain, pain ever, for ever. Like thee, Prometheus, no change, no pause, no hope. Ah, life, life, life! (*There is a gentle knock at the door.*) Another Fury come to plague me now!

> [*Another knock, a little louder.*

Davoren. You can knock till you're tired.

> [*The door opens and* Minnie Powell *enters with an easy confidence one would not expect her to possess from her gentle way of knocking. She is a girl of twenty-three, but the fact of being forced to earn her living, and to take care of herself, on account of her parents' early death, has given her a force and an assurance beyond her years. She has lost the sense of fear (she does not know this), and, consequently, she is at ease in all places and before all*

persons, even those of a superior education, so long as she meets them in the atmosphere that surrounds the members of her own class. Her hair is brown, neither light nor dark, but partaking of both tints according to the light or shade she may happen to be in. Her well-shaped figure— a rare thing in a city girl—is charmingly dressed in a brown tailor-made costume, her stockings and shoes are a darker brown tint than the costume, and all are crowned by a silk tam-o'shanter of a rich blue tint.

Minnie. Are you in, Mr. Shields?

Davoren (rapidly). No, he's not, Minnie; he's just gone out—if you run out quickly you're sure to catch him.

Minnie. Oh, it's all right, Mr. Davoren, you'll do just as well; I just come in for a drop o' milk for a cup o' tea; I shouldn't be troublin' you this way, but I'm sure you don't mind.

Davoren (dubiously). No trouble in the world; delighted, I'm sure. *(Giving her the milk.)* There, will you have enough?

Minnie. Plenty, lashins, thanks. Do you be all alone all the day, Mr. Davoren?

Davoren. No, indeed; I wish to God I was.

Minnie. It's not good for you then. I don't know how you like to be by yourself—I couldn't stick it long.

Davoren (wearily). No?

Minnie. No, indeed; *(with rapture)* there's nothin' I'm more fond of than a Hooley. I was at one last Sunday—I danced rings round me! Tommy Owens was there—you know Tommy Owens, don't you?

Davoren. I can't say I do.

Minnie. D'ye not? The little fellow that lives with his mother in the two-pair back—*(ecstatically)* he's a gorgeous melodeon player!

Davoren. A gifted son of Orpheus, eh?

Minnie (who never heard of Orpheus). You've said it, Mr. Davoren: the son of poor oul' Battie Owens, a weeshy, dawny, bit of a man that was never sober an' was always talkin' politics. Poor man, it killed him in the long run.

Davoren. A man should always be drunk, Minnie, when he talks politics—it's the only way in which to make them important.

Minnie. Tommy takes after the oul' fellow, too; he'd talk from morning till night when he has a few jars in him. (*Suddenly; for like all of her class, Minnie is not able to converse very long on the one subject, and her thoughts spring from one thing to another.*) Poetry is a grand thing, Mr. Davoren, I'd love to be able to write a poem—a lovely poem on Ireland an' the men o' '98.

Davoren. Oh, we've had enough of poems, Minnie, about '98, and of Ireland, too.

Minnie. Oh, there's a thing for a Republican to say! But I know what you mean: it's time to give up the writing an' take to the gun. (*Her roving eye catches sight of the flowers in the vase.*) What's Mr. Shields doin' with the oul' weeds?

Davoren. Those aren't Shields', they're mine. Wild flowers is a kindlier name for them, Minnie, than weeds. These are wild violets, this is an *Arum maculatum*, or Wake Robin, and these are Celandines, a very beautiful flower related to the buttercups. (*He quotes*):

> One day, when Morn's half-open'd eyes
> Were bright with Spring sunshine—
> My hand was clasp'd in yours, dear love,
> And yours was clasp'd in mine—
> We bow'd as worshippers before
> The Golden Celandine.

Minnis. Oh, aren't they lovely, an' isn't the poem lovely, too! I wonder, now, who she was.

Davoren (*puzzled*). She, who?

Minnie. Why, the . . . (*roguishly*) Oh, be the way you don't know.

Davoren. Know? I'm sure I don't know.

Minnie. It doesn't matter, anyhow—that's your own business; I suppose I don't know her.

Davoren. Know her—know whom?

Minnie (shyly). Her whose hand was clasped in yours, an' yours was clasped in hers.

Davoren. Oh, that—that was simply a poem I quoted about the Celandine, that might apply to any girl—to you, for instance.

Minnie (greatly relieved, coming over and sitting beside Davoren). But you have a sweetheart, all the same, Mr. Davoren, haven't you?

Davoren. I? No, not one, Minnie.

Minnie. Oh, now, you can tell that to some one else; aren't you a poet an' aren't all the girls fond o' poets?

Davoren. That may be, but all the poets aren't fond of girls.

Minnie. They are in the story-books, ay, and fond of more than one, too. (*With a questioning look*) Are you fond of them, Mr. Davoren?

Davoren. Of course I like girls, Minnie, especially girls who can add to their charms by the way in which they dress, like you, for instance.

Minnie. Oh, now, you're on for coddin' me, Mr. Davoren.

Davoren. No, really, Minnie, I'm not; you are a very charming little girl indeed.

Minnie. Then if I'm a charmin' little girl, you ought to be able to write a poem about me.

Davoren (who has become susceptible to the attractiveness of Minnie, catching her hand). And so I will, so I will, Minnie; I have written them about girls not half so pretty as yourself.

Minnie. Ah, I knew you had one, I knew you had one now.

Davoren. Nonsense. Every girl a poet writes about isn't his sweetheart; Annie Laurie wasn't the sweetheart of Bobbie Burns.

Minnie. You needn't tell me she wasn't; 'An' for bonnie Annie Laurie I'd lay me down an' die'. No man ud lay down an' die for any but a sweetheart, not even for a wife.

Davoren. No man, Minnie, willingly dies for anything.

Minnie. Except for his country, like Robert Emmet.

Davoren. Even he would have lived on if he could; he died not to deliver Ireland. The British Government killed him to save the British nation.

Minnie. You're only jokin' now; you'd die for your country.

Davoren. I don't know so much about that.

Minnie. You would, you would, you would—I know what you are.

Davoren. What am I?

Minnie (in a whisper). A gunman on the run!

Davoren (too pleased to deny it). Maybe I am, and maybe I'm not.

Minnie. Oh, I know, I know, I know. Do you never be afraid?

Davoren. Afraid! Afraid of what?

Minnie. Why, the ambushes of course; *I'm* all of a tremble when I hear a shot go off, an' what must it be in the middle of the firin'?

Davoren (delighted at Minnie's *obvious admiration; leaning back in his chair, and lighting a cigarette with placid affectation).* I'll admit one does be a little nervous at first, but a fellow gets used to it after a bit, till, at last, a gunman throws a bomb as carelessly as a schoolboy throws a snowball.

Minnie (fervently). I wish it was all over, all the same. *(Suddenly, with a tremor in her voice.)* You'll take care of yourself, won't you, won't you, Donal—I mean, Mr. Davoren?

Davoren (earnestly). Call me Donal, Minnie; we're friends, great friends now—*(putting his arm around her)* go on, Minnie, call me Donal, let me hear you say Donal.

Minnie. The place badly needs a tidyin' up . . . Donal

—there now, are you satisfied? (*Rapidly, half afraid of Davoren's excited emotions.*) But it really does, it's in an awful state. To-morrow's a half-day, an' I'll run in an' straighten it up a bit.

Davoren (*frightened at the suggestion*). No, no, Minnie, you're too pretty for that sort of work; besides, the people of the house would be sure to start talking about you.

Minnie. An' do you think Minnie Powell cares whether they'll talk or no? She's had to push her way through life up to this without help from any one, an' she's not goin' to ask their leave, now, to do what she wants to do.

Davoren (*forgetting his timidity in the honest joy of appreciating the independent courage of Minnie*). My soul within art thou, Minnie! A pioneer in action as I am a pioneer in thought. The two powers that shall 'grasp this sorry scheme of things entire, and mould life nearer to the heart's desire'. Lovely little Minnie, and brave as well; brave little Minnie, and lovely as well!

> [*His disengaged hand lifts up her bent head, and he looks earnestly at her; he is stooping to kiss her, when* Tommy Owens *appears at the door, which* Minnie *has left partially open.* Tommy *is about twenty-five years of age. He is small and thin; his words are uttered in a nasal drawl; his voice is husky, due to frequent drinks and perpetual cigarette-smoking. He tries to get rid of the huskiness by an occasional cough.* Tommy *is a hero-worshipper, and, like many others, he is anxious to be on familiar terms with those who he thinks are braver than he is himself, and whose approbation he tries to win by an assumption equal to their own. He talks in a staccato manner. He has a few drinks taken—it is too early to be drunk—that make him talkative. He is dressed in a suit of dungarees, and gives a gentle cough to draw attention to his presence.*

Tommy. I seen nothin'—honest—thought you was learnin'

to typewrite—Mr. Davoren teachin' you. I seen nothin'
else—s'help me God!

Minnie. We'd be hard put to it if we minded what you
seen, Tommy Owens.

Tommy. Right, Minnie, Tommy Owens has a heart—
Evenin', Mr. Davoren—don't mind me comin' in—I'm
Tommy Owens—live up in the two-pair back, workin' in
Ross an' Walpole's—Mr. Shields knows me well; you needn't
be afraid o' me, Mr. Davoren.

Davoren. Why should I be afraid of you, Mr. Owens, or
of anybody else?

Tommy. Why should you, indeed? We're all friends
here—Mr. Shields knows me well—all you've got to say is,
'Do you know Tommy Owens?' an' he'll tell you the sort of a
man Tommy Owens is. There's no flies on Tommy—got me?

Minnie. For goodness' sake, Tommy, leave Mr. Davoren
alone—he's got enough burgeons on him already.

Tommy. Not a word, Minnie, not a word—Mr. Davoren
understands me well, as man to man. It's 'Up the Republic' all the time—eh, Mr. Davoren?

Davoren. I know nothing about the Republic; I have no
connection with the politics of the day, and I don't want to
have any connection.

Tommy. You needn't say no more—a nod's as good as
a wink to a blind horse—you've no meddlin' or makin' with
it, good, bad, or indifferent, pro nor con; I know it an'
Minnie knows it—give me your hand. (*He catches* Davoren's
hand.) Two firm hands clasped together will all the power
outbrave of the heartless English tyrant, the Saxon coward an'
knave. That's Tommy Owens' hand, Mr. Davoren, the hand
of a man, a man—Mr. Shields knows me well.

[*He breaks into song.*

High upon the gallows tree stood the noble-hearted three,
By the vengeful tyrant stricken in their bloom;

But they met him face to face with the spirit of their race,
And they went with souls undaunted to their doom!

Minnie (in an effort to quell his fervour). Tommy Owens, for
goodness' sake . . .

Tommy (overwhelming her with a shout):

God save Ireland ses the hayros, God save Ireland ses we all,
Whether on the scaffold high or the battle-field we die.
Oh, what matter when for Ayryinn dear we fall!

(Tearfully) Mr. Davoren, I'd die for Ireland!

Davoren. I know you would, I know you would, Tommy.

Tommy. I never got a chance—they never gave me a
chance—but all the same I'd be there if I was called on—Mr.
Shields knows that—ask Mr. Shields, Mr. Davoren.

Davoren. There's no necessity, Tommy; I know you're
the right stuff if you got the chance, but remember that 'he
also serves who only stands and waits'.

Tommy (fiercely). I'm bloody well tired o' waitin'—we're
all tired o' waitin'. Why isn't every man in Ireland out with
the I.R.A.? Up with the barricades, up with the barricades;
it's now or never, now an' for ever, as Sarsfield said at the
battle o' Vinegar Hill. Up with the barricades—that's
Tommy Owens—an' a penny buys a whistle. Let them as
thinks different say different—what do you say, Mr. Davoren?

Davoren. I say, Tommy, you ought to go up and get your
dinner, for if you wait much longer it won't be worth eating.

Tommy. Oh, damn the dinner; who'd think o' dinner an'
Ireland fightin' to be free—not Tommy Owens, anyhow. It's
only the Englishman who's always thinkin' of his belly.

Minnie. Tommy Owens!

Tommy. Excuse me, Miss Powell, in the ardure ov me
anger I disremembered there was a lady present.

> [*Voices are heard outside, and presently* Mrs. Henderson
> *comes into the room, followed by* Mr. Gallogher, *who*

*however, lingers at the door, too timid to come any further.
Mrs. Henderson is a massive woman in every way;
massive head, arms, and body; massive voice, and a
massive amount of self-confidence. She is a mountain of
good nature, and during the interview she behaves towards
Davoren with deferential self-assurance. She dominates
the room, and seems to occupy the whole of it. She is
dressed poorly but tidily, wearing a white apron and a
large shawl. Mr. Gallogher, on the other hand, is a spare
little man with a spare little grey beard and a thin, nervous
voice. He is dressed as well as a faded suit of blue will
allow him to be. He is obviously ill at ease during his
interview with Davoren. He carries a hard hat, much
the worse for wear, under his left arm, and a letter in his right
hand.*

Mrs. Henderson (entering the room). Come along in, Mr.
Gallicker, Mr. Davoren won't mind; it's him as can put you
in the way o' havin' your wrongs righted; come on in, man,
an' don't be so shy—Mr. Davoren is wan ov ourselves that
stands for govermint ov the people with the people by the
people. You'll find you'll be as welcome as the flowers in
May. Good evenin', Mr. Davoren, an' God an' His holy
angels be between you an' all harm.

Tommy (effusively). Come on, Mr. Gallicker, an' don't be
a stranger—we're all friends here—anything special to be done
or particular advice asked, here's your man here.

*Davoren (subconsciously pleased, but a little timid of the belief
that he is connected with the gunmen).* I'm very busy just now, Mrs.
Henderson, and really . . .

Mrs. Henderson (mistaking the reason of his embarrassment).
Don't be put out, Mr. Davoren, we won't keep you more nor
a few minutes. It's not in me or in Mr. Gallicker to spoil
sport. Him an' me was young once, an' knows what it is to
be strolling at night in the pale moonlight, with arms round one
another. An' I wouldn't take much an' say there's game in

Mr. Gallicker still, for I seen, sometimes, a dangerous cock in his eye. But we won't keep you an' Minnie long asunder; he's the letter an' all written. You must know, Mr. Davoren —excuse me for not introducin' him sooner—this is Mr. Gallicker, that lives in the front drawin'-room ov number fifty-five, as decent an' honest an' quiet a man as you'd meet in a day's walk. An' so signs on it, it's them as 'ill be imposed upon—read the letter, Mr. Gallicker.

Tommy. Read away, Mr. Gallicker, it will be attended to, never fear; we know our own know, eh, Mr. Davoren?

Minnie. Hurry up, Mr. Gallicker, an' don't be keeping Mr. Davoren.

Mrs. Henderson. Give him time, Minnie Powell. Give him time. You must know in all fairity, Mr. Davoren, that the family livin' in the next room to Mr. Gallicker—the back drawin'-room, to be particular—am I right or am I wrong, Mr. Gallicker?

Mr. Gallogher. You're right, Mrs. Henderson, perfectly right, indeed—that's the very identical room.

Mrs. Henderson. Well, Mr. Davoren, the people in the back drawin'-room, or, to be more particular, the residents— that's the word that's writ in the letter—am I right or am I wrong, Mr. Gallicker?

Mr. Gallogher. You're right, Mrs. Henderson, perfectly accurate—that's the very identical word.

Mrs. Henderson. Well, Mr. Davoren, the residents in the back drawin'-room, as I aforesaid, is nothin' but a gang o' tramps that oughtn't to be allowed to associate with honest, decent, quiet, respectable people. Mr. Gallicker has tried to reason with them, and make them behave themselves—which in my opinion they never will—however, that's only an opinion, an' not legal—ever since they have made Mr. Gallicker's life a HELL! Mr. Gallicker, am I right or am I wrong?

Mr. Gallogher. I'm sorry to say you're right, Mrs. Henderson, perfectly right—not a word of exaggeration.

Mrs. Henderson. Well, now, Mr. Gallicker, seein' as I have given Mr. Davoren a fair account ov how you're situated, an' ov these tramps' cleverality, I'll ask you to read the letter, which I'll say, not because you're there, or that you're a friend o' mine, is as good a letter as was decomposed by a scholar. Now, Mr. Gallicker, an' don't forget the top sayin'.

> [Mr. Gallogher *prepares to read;* Minnie *leans forward to listen;* Tommy *takes out a well-worn note-book and a pencil stump, and assumes a very important attitude.*

Tommy. One second. Mr. Gallicker, is this the twenty-first or twenty-second?

Mr. Gallogher. The twenty-first, sir.

Tommy. Thanks; proceed, Mr. Gallicker.

Mr. Gallogher (with a few preliminary tremors, reads the letter. Reading):

'To All to Whom These Presents Come,
    Greeting

'Gentlemen of the Irish Republican Army . . .'

Mrs. Henderson. There's a beginnin' for you, Mr. Davoren.

Minnie. That's some swank.

Tommy. There's a lot in that sayin', mind you; it's a hard wallop at the British Empire.

Mrs. Henderson (proudly). Go on, Mr. Gallicker.

Mr. Gallogher (reading):

'I wish to call your attention to the persecution me and my family has to put up with in respect of and appertaining to the residents of the back drawing-room of the house known as fifty-five, Saint Teresa Street, situate in the Parish of St. Thomas, in the Borough and City of Dublin. This persecution started eighteen months ago—or to be precise—on the tenth day of the sixth month, in the year nineteen hundred and twenty.'

Mrs. Henderson. That's the word I was trying to think ov
—precise—it cuts the ground from under their feet—so to
speak.

Mr. Gallogher (reading):

'We, the complainants, resident on the ground floor,
deeming it disrespectable . . .'

Mrs. Henderson (with an emphatic nod). Which it was.

Mr. Gallogher (reading):

'Deeming it disrespectable to have an open hall door,
and to have the hall turned into a playground, made a
solemn protest, and, in consequence, we the complainants
aforesaid has had no peace ever since. Owing to the persecution, as aforesaid specified, we had to take out a summons
again them some time ago as there was no Republican
Courts then; but we did not proceed again them as me and
my wife—to wit, James and Winifred Gallogher—has a
strong objection to foreign Courts as such. We had peace
for some time after that, but now things have gone from
bad to worse. The name calling and the language is something abominable . . .'

*Mrs. Henderson (holding out her hand as a constable would extend
his to stop a car that another may pass).* Excuse me, Mr. Gallicker,
but I think the word 'shockin'' should be put in there after
abominable; for the language used be these tramps has two
ways o' bein' looked at—for it's abominable to the childer an'
shockin' to your wife—am I right or am I wrong, Mr.
Davoren?

Tommy (judicially). Shockin' is a right good word, with a
great deal o' meanin', an' . . .

*Mrs. Henderson (with a deprecating gesture that extinguishes
Tommy).* Tommy, let Mr. Davoren speak; whatever Mr.
Davoren ses, Julia Henderson'll abide be.

Davoren (*afraid to say anything else*).   I think the word might certainly be introduced with advantage.

Mrs. Henderson.   Go over there, Mr. Gallicker, an' put in the word shockin', as aforesaid.

> [Gallogher *goes over to the table, and with a great deal of difficulty enters the word.*

Tommy (*to* Mr. Gallogher *as he writes*).   Ey, there's two k's in shockin'!

Mr. Gallogher (*reading*):

'The language is something abominable and shocking. My wife has often to lock the door of the room to keep them from assaulting her.   If you would be so kind as to send some of your army or police down to see for themselves we would give them full particulars.   I have to be always from home all day, as I work with Mr. Hennessy, the harness maker of the Coombe, who will furnish all particulars as to my unvarnished respectability, also my neighbours.   The name of the resident-tenant who is giving all this trouble and who, pursuant to the facts of the case aforesaid, mentioned, will be the defendant, is Dwyer.   The husband of the aforesaid Mrs. Dwyer, or the aforesaid defendant, as the case may be, is a seaman, who is coming home shortly, and we beg The Irish Republican Army to note that the said Mrs. Dwyer says he will settle us when he comes home. While leaving it entirely in the hands of the gentlemen of The Republican Army, the defendant, that is to say, James Gallogher of fifty-five St. Teresa Street, ventures to say that he thinks he has made out a Primmy Fashy Case against Mrs. Dwyer and all her heirs, male and female as aforesaid mentioned in the above written schedule.

'*N.B.*—If you send up any of your men, please tell them to bring their guns.   I beg to remain the humble servant and devoted admirer of the Gentlemen of the Irish Republican Army.

'Witness my hand this tenth day of the fifth month of the year nineteen hundred and twenty.

'JAMES GALLOGHER.'

Mr. Gallogher (with a modest cough). Ahem.

Mrs. Henderson. There's a letter for you, Mr. Davoren!

Tommy. It's the most powerfullest letter I ever heard read.

Minnie. It wasn't you, really, that writ it, Mr. Gallicker?

Mrs. Henderson. Sinn Fein Amhain: him an' him only, Minnie. I seen him with me own two eyes when me an' Winnie—Mrs. Gallicker, Mr. Davoren, aforesaid as appears in the letter—was havin' a chat be the fire.

Minnie. You'd never think it was in him to do it.

Mrs. Henderson. An' to think that the likes ov such a man is to have the sowl-case worried out ov him by a gang o' tramps; but it's in good hands now, an' instead ov them settlin' yous, Mr. Gallicker, it's yous 'ill settle them. Give the letter to Mr. Davoren, an' we'll be goin'.

[Gallogher *gives the letter to* Davoren.

Mrs. Henderson (moving towards the door). I hope you an' Mr. Shields is gettin' on all right together, Mr. Davoren.

Davoren. Fairly well, thanks, Mrs. Henderson. We don't see much of each other. He's out during the day, and I'm usually out during the evening.

Mrs. Henderson. I'm afraid he'll never make a fortune out ov what he's sellin'. He'll talk above an hour over a pennorth o' pins. Every time he comes to our place I buy a package o' hairpins from him to give him a little encouragement. I 'clare to God I have as many pins now as ud make a wire mattress for a double bed. All the young divils about the place are beginnin' to make a jeer ov him, too; I gave one ov them a mallavogin' the other day for callin' him oul' hairpins!

Mr. Gallogher (venturing an opinion). Mr. Shields is a man of exceptional mental capacity, and is worthy of a more dignified position.

Mrs. Henderson. Them words is true, Mr. Gallicker, and they aren't. For to be wise is to be a fool, an' to be a fool is to be wise.

Mr. Gallogher (with deprecating tolerance). Oh, Mrs. Henderson, that's a parrotox.

Mrs. Henderson. It may be what a parrot talks, or a blackbird, or, for the matter of that, a lark—but it's what Julia Henderson thinks, any . . . whisht, is that a *Stop Press*?

[*Outside is heard the shriek of a newsboy calling 'Stop Press'.*]

Mrs. Henderson. Run out, Tommy, an' get it till we see what it is.

Tommy. I haven't got a make.

Mrs. Henderson. I never seen you any other way, an' you'll be always the same if you keep follyin' your Spearmints, an' your Bumble Bees an' your Night Patrols. (*Shouting to someone outside*) Is that a *Stop Press*, Mrs. Grigson?

Voice outside. Yis; an ambush out near Knocksedan.

Mrs. Henderson. That's the stuff to give them. (*Loudly*) Was there anybody hurted?

Voice outside. One poor man killed—some chap named Maguire, the paper says.

Davoren (agitated). What name did she say?

Minnie. Maguire; did you know him, Mr. Davoren?

Davoren. Yes—no, no; I didn't know him, no, I didn't know him, Minnie.

Minnie. I wonder is it the Maguire that does be with Mr. Shields?

Davoren. Oh no, not at all, it couldn't be.

Mrs. Henderson. Knocksedan? That's in the County Sligo, now, or I'm greatly mistaken—am I right, Mr. Gallicker, or am I wrong?

Mr. Gallogher (who knows perfectly well that it is in the County Dublin, but dare not correct Mrs. Henderson). That's where it is—Knocksedan, that's the very identical county.

Mrs. Henderson. Well, I think we better be makin' a

move, Mr. Gallicker; we've kep' Mr. Davoren long enough, an' you'll find the letter'll be in good hans.

[*Mr. Gallogher and* Mrs. Henderson *move towards the door, which when he reaches it* Mr. Gallogher *grips, hesitates, buttons his coat, and turns to* Davoren.

Mr. Gallogher. Mr. Davoren, sir, on behalf ov meself, James Gallicker, an' Winifred, Mrs. Gallicker, wife ov the said James, I beg to offer, extend an' furnish our humble an' hearty thanks for your benevolent goodness in interferin' in the matter specified, particularated an' expanded upon in the letter, mandamus or schedule, as the case may be. An' let me interpretate to you on behalf ov meself an' Winifred Gallicker, that whenever you visit us you will be supernally positive ov a hundred thousand welcomes—ahem.

Mrs. Henderson (*beaming with pride for the genius of her friend*). There's a man for you, Mr. Davoren! You forgot to mention Biddy and Shaun, Mr. Gallicker—(*to* Davoren) his two children—it's himself has them trained well. It ud make your heart thrill like an alarm clock to hear them singin' 'Faith ov Our Fathers' an' 'Wrap the Green Flag Roun me'.

Mr. Gallogher (*half apologetically and half proudly*). Faith an' Fatherland, Mrs. Henderson, Faith and Fatherland.

Mrs. Henderson. Well, good-day, Mr. Davoren, an' God keep you an' strengthen all the men that are fightin' for Ireland's freedom. [*She and* Gallogher *go out.*

Tommy. I must be off too; so-long, Mr. Davoren, an' remember that Tommy Owens only waits the call.

[*He goes out too.*

Davoren. Well, Minnie, we're by ourselves once more.

Minnie. Wouldn't that Tommy Owens give you the sick—only waitin' to hear the call! Ah, then it'll take all the brass bands in the country to blow the call before Tommy Owens ud hear it. (*She looks at her wristlet watch.*) Sacred Heart, I've only ten minutes to get back to work! I'll have to fly!

Quick, Mr. Davoren, write me name in typewritin' before I go—just 'Minnie'.   [*Davoren types the name.*

Minnie (*shyly but determinedly*). Now yours underneath—just 'Donal'. (Davoren *does so.*) Minnie, Donal; Donal, Minnie; good-bye now.

Davoren. Here, what about your milk?

Minnie. I haven't time to take it now. (*Slyly*) I'll come for it this evening.   [*They both go towards the door.*

Davoren. Minnie, the kiss I didn't get.

Minnie. What kiss?

Davoren. When we were interrupted; you know, you little rogue, come, just one.

Minnie. Quick, then.

        [*Davoren kisses her and she runs out.* Davoren *returns thoughtfully to the table.*

Davoren. Minnie, Donal; Donal, Minnie. Very pretty, but very ignorant. A gunman on the run! Be careful, be careful, Donal Davoren. But Minnie is attracted to the idea, and I am attracted to Minnie. And what danger can there be in being the shadow of a gunman?

CURTAIN

ACT II

*The same as in Act I. But it is now night. Seumas is in the
bed that runs along the wall at back. Davoren is seated near the
fire, to which he has drawn the table. He has a fountain-pen in his
hand, and is attracted in thought towards the moon, which is shining
in through the windows. An open writing-pad is on the table at
Davoren's elbow. The bag left by Maguire is still in the same
place.*

Davoren:

    The cold chaste moon, the Queen of Heaven's bright isles,
    Who makes all beautiful on which she smiles;
    That wandering shrine of soft yet icy flame,
    Which ever is transformed yet still the same.

Ah, Shelley, Shelley, you yourself were a lovely human
orb shining through clouds of whirling human dust. 'She
makes all beautiful on which she smiles.' Ah, Shelley,
she couldn't make this thrice accursed room beautiful. Her
beams of beauty only make its horrors more full of horrors
still. There is an ugliness that can be made beautiful, and
there is an ugliness that can only be destroyed, and this is part
of that ugliness. Donal, Donal, I fear your last state is worse
than your first.

       [He lilts a verse, which he writes on the pad before him.

    When night advances through the sky with slow
      And solemn tread.
    The queenly moon looks down on life below,
      As if she read
    Man's soul, and in her scornful silence said:
      All beautiful and happiest things are dead.

Seumas (*sleepily*). Donal, Donal, are you awake? (*A pause.*) Donal, Donal, are you asleep?

Davoren. I'm neither awake nor asleep: I'm thinking.

Seumas. I was just thinkin', too—I was just thinkin', too, that Maguire is sorry now that he didn't come with me instead of going to Knocksedan. He caught something besides butterflies—two of them he got, one through each lung.

Davoren. The Irish people are very fond of turning a serious thing into a joke; that was a serious affair—for poor Maguire.

Seumas (*defensively*). Why didn't he do what he arranged to do? Did he think of me when he was goin' to Knocksedan? How can he expect me to have any sympathy with him now?

Davoren. He can hardly expect that now that he's dead.

Seumas. The Republicans 'll do a lot for him, now. How am I goin' to get back the things he has belongin' to me, either? There's some of them in that bag over there, but that's not quarter of what he had; an' I don't know where he was stoppin', for he left his old digs a week or so ago—I suppose there's nothing to be said about my loss; I'm to sing dumb.

Davoren. I hope there's nothing else in the bag, besides thread and hairpins.

Seumas. What else ud be in it? . . . I can't sleep properly ever since they put on this damned curfew. A minute ago I thought I heard some of the oul' ones standin' at the door; they won't be satisfied till they bring a raid on the house; an' they never begin to stand at the door till after curfew. . . . Are you gone to bed, Donal?

Davoren. No; I'm trying to finish this poem.

Seumas (*sitting up in bed*). If I was you I'd give that game up; it doesn't pay a working-man to write poetry. I don't profess to know much about poetry—I don't profess to know much about poetry—about poetry—I don't know much about the pearly glint of the morning dew, or the damask sweetness of the rare wild rose, or the subtle greenness of the serpent's eye—but I think a poet's claim to greatness depends upon his power to put passion in the common people.

Davoren. Ay, passion to howl for his destruction. The People! Damn the people! They live in the abyss, the poet lives on the mountain-top; to the people there is no mystery of colour: it is simply the scarlet coat of the soldier; the purple vestments of a priest; the green banner of a party; the brown or blue overalls of industry. To them the might of design is a three-roomed house or a capacious bed. To them beauty is for sale in a butcher's shop. To the people the end of life is the life created for them; to the poet the end of life is the life that he creates for himself; life has a stifling grip upon the people's throat—it is the poet's musician. The poet ever strives to save the people; the people ever strive to destroy the poet. The people view life through creeds, through customs, and through necessities; the poet views creeds, customs, and necessities through life. The people . . .

Seumas (*suddenly, and with a note of anxiety in his voice*). Whisht! What's that? Is that the tappin' again?

Davoren. Tappin'. What tappin'?

Seumas (*in an awed whisper*). This is the second night I heard that tappin! I believe it bodes no good to me. There, do you hear it again—a quiet, steady, mysterious tappin' on the wall.

Davoren. I hear no tappin'.

Seumas. It ud be better for me if you did. It's a sure sign of death when nobody hears it but meself.

Davoren. Death! What the devil are you talking about, man?

Seumas. I don't like it at all; there's always something like that heard when one of our family dies.

Davoren. I don't know about that; but I know there's a hell of a lot of things heard when one of your family lives.

Seumas. God between us an' all harm! Thank God I'm where I ought to be—in bed. . . . It's always best to be in your proper place when such things happen—Sacred Heart! There it is again; do you not hear it now?

Davoren. Ah, for God's sake go asleep.

Seumas. Do you believe in nothing?

Davoren. I don't believe in tappin'.

Seumas. Whisht, it's stopped again; I'll try to go asleep for fear it ud begin again.

Davoren. Ay, do; and if it starts again I'll be sure to waken you up.   [*A pause.*

Seumas. It's very cold to-night. Do you feel cold?

Davoren. I thought you were goin' asleep?

Seumas. The bloody cold won't let me. . . . You'd want a pair of pyjamas on you. (*A pause.*) Did you ever wear pyjamas, Donal?

Davoren. No, no, no.

Seumas. What kind of stuff is in them?

Davoren (*angrily*). Oh, it depends on the climate; in India, silk; in Italy, satin; and the Eskimo wears them made from the skin of the Polar bear.

Seumas (*emphatically*). If you take my advice you'll get into bed—that poem is beginnin' to get on your nerves.

Davoren (*extinguishing the candle with a vicious blow*). Right; I'm going to bed now, so you can shut up.

                    [*Visibility is still maintained from the light of the moon.*

Seumas. I was goin' to say something when you put out the light—what's this it was?—um, um, oh, ay: when I was comin' in this evenin' I saw Minnie Powell goin' out. If I was you I wouldn't have that one comin' in here.

Davoren. She comes in; I don't bring her in, do I?

Seumas. The oul' ones'll be talkin', an' once they start you don't know how it'll end. Surely a man that has read Shelley couldn't be interested in an ignorant little bitch that thinks of nothin' but jazz dances, fox-trots, picture theatres an' dress.

Davoren. Right glad I am that she thinks of dress, for she thinks of it in the right way, and makes herself a pleasant picture to the eye. Education has been wasted on many persons, teaching them to talk only, but leaving them with all their primitive instincts. Had poor Minnie received an education she would have been an artist. She is certainly a pretty girl. I'm sure she is a good girl, and I believe she is a brave girl.

Seumas. A Helen of Troy come to live in a tenement! You think a lot about her simply because she thinks a lot about you, an' she thinks a lot about you because she looks upon you as a hero—a kind o' Paris . . . she'd give the world an' all to be gaddin' about with a gunman. An' what ecstasy it ud give her if after a bit you were shot or hanged; she'd be able to go about then—like a good many more—singin', 'I do not mourn me darlin' lost, for he fell in his Jacket Green'. An' then, for a year an' a day, all round her hat she'd wear the Tricoloured Ribbon O, till she'd pick up an' marry someone else —possibly a British Tommy with a Mons Star. An' as for bein' brave, it's easy to be that when you've no cause for cowardice; I wouldn't care to have me life dependin' on brave little Minnie Powell—she wouldn't sacrifice a jazz dance to save it.

Davoren (*sitting on the bed and taking off his coat and vest, preparatory to going to bed*). There; that's enough about Minnie Powell. I'm afraid I'll soon have to be on the run out of this house, too; it is becoming painfully obvious that there is no peace to be found here.

Seumas. Oh, this house is all right; barrin' the children, it does be quiet enough. Wasn't there children in the last place you were in too?

Davoren. Ay, ten; (*viciously*) and they were all over forty.
　　　　　　[*A pause as* Davoren *is removing his collar and tie.*

Seumas. Everything is very quiet now; I wonder what time is it?

Davoren. The village cock hath thrice done salutation to the morn.

Seumas. Shakespeare, Richard the III, Act Five, Scene III. It was Ratcliff said that to Richard just before the battle of Bosworth. . . . How peaceful the heavens look now with the moon in the middle; you'd never think there were men prowlin' about tryin' to shoot each other. I don't know how a man who has shot any one can sleep in peace at night.

Davoren. There's plenty of men can't sleep in peace at night now unless they know that they have shot somebody.

Seumas. I wish to God it was all over. The country is gone mad. Instead of counting their beads now they're countin' bullets; their Hail Marys and paternosters are burstin' bombs—burstin' bombs, an' the rattle of machine-guns; petrol is their holy water; their Mass is a burnin' buildin'; their De Profundis is 'The Soldiers' Song', an' their creed is, I believe in the gun almighty, maker of heaven an' earth—an' it's all for 'the glory o' God an' the honour o' Ireland'.

Davoren. I remember the time when you yourself believed in nothing but the gun.

Seumas. Ay, when there wasn't a gun in the country; I've a different opinion now when there's nothin' but guns in the country. . . . An' you daren't open your mouth, for Kathleen ni Houlihan is very different now to the woman who used to play the harp an' sing 'Weep on, weep on, your hour is past', for she's a ragin' divil now, an' if you only look crooked at her you're sure of a punch in th' eye. But this is the way I look at it—I look at it this way: You're not goin'—you're not goin' to beat the British Empire—the British Empire, by shootin' an occasional Tommy at the corner of an occasional street. Besides, when the Tommies have the wind up—when the Tommies have the wind up they let bang at everything they see—they don't give a God's curse who they plug.

Davoren. Maybe they ought to get down off the lorry and

run to the Records Office to find out a man's pedigree before they plug him.

Seumas. It's the civilians that suffer; when there's an ambush they don't know where to run. Shot in the back to save the British Empire, an' shot in the breast to save the soul of Ireland. I'm a Nationalist meself, right enough—a Nationalist right enough, but all the same—I'm a Nationalist right enough; I believe in the freedom of Ireland, an' that England has no right to be here, but I draw the line when I hear the gunmen blowin' about dyin' for the people, when it's the people that are dyin' for the gunmen! With all due respect to the gunmen, I don't want them to die for me.

Davoren. Not likely; you object to any one of them deliberately dying for you for fear that one of these days you might accidentally die for one of them.

Seumas. You're one of the brave fellows that doesn't fear death.

Davoren. Why should I be afraid of it? It's all the same to me how it comes, where it comes, or when it comes. I leave fear of death to the people that are always praying for eternal life; 'Death is here and death is there, death is busy everywhere'.

Seumas. Ay, in Ireland. Thanks be to God I'm a daily communicant. There's a great comfort in religion; it makes a man strong in time of trouble an' brave in time of danger. No man need be afraid with a crowd of angels round him; thanks to God for His Holy religion!

Davoren. You're welcome to your angels; philosophy is mine; philosophy that makes the coward brave; the sufferer defiant; the weak strong; the . . .

   [*A volley of shots is heard in a lane that runs parallel with the wall of the back-yard. Religion and philosophy are forgotten in the violent fear of a nervous equality.*

Seumas. Jesus, Mary, an' Joseph, what's that?

Davoren. My God, that's very close.

Seumas. Is there no Christianity at all left in the country?

Davoren. Are we ever again going to know what peace and security are?

Seumas. If this continues much longer I'll be nothing but a galvanic battery o' shocks.

Davoren. It's dangerous to be in and it's equally dangerous to be out.

Seumas. This is a dangerous spot to be in with them windows; you couldn't tell the minute a bullet ud come in through one of them—through one of them, an' hit the—hit the—an' hit the . . .

Davoren (*irritably*). Hit the what, man?

Seumas. The wall.

Davoren. Couldn't you say that at first without making a song about it?

Seumas (*suddenly*). I don't believe there's horses in the stable at all.

Davoren. Stable! What stable are you talking about?

Seumas. There's a stable at the back of the house with an entrance from the yard; it's used as a carpenter's shop. Didn't you often hear the peculiar noises at night? They give out that it's the horses shakin' their chains.

Davoren. And what is it?

Seumas. Oh, there I'll leave you!

Davoren. Surely you don't mean . . .

Seumas. But I do mean it.

Davoren. You do mean what?

Seumas. I wouldn't—I wouldn't be surprised—wouldn't be surprised—surprised . . .

Davoren. Yes, yes, surprised—go on.

Seumas. I wouldn't be surprised if they were manufacturin' bombs there.

Davoren. My God, that's a pleasant contemplation! The sooner I'm on the run out of this house the better. How is it you never said anything about this before?

Seumas. Well—well, I didn't want—I didn't want to—to . . .

Davoren. You didn't want to what?

Seumas. I didn't want to frighten you.

Davoren (sarcastically). You're bloody kind!

[*A knock at the door; the voice of* Mrs. Grigson *heard.*

Mrs. Grigson. Are you asleep, Mr. Shields?

Seumas. What the devil can she want at this hour of the night? (*To* Mrs. Grigson) No, Mrs. Grigson, what is it?

Mrs. Grigson (opening the door and standing at the threshold. She is a woman about forty, but looks much older. She is one of the cave dwellers of Dublin, living as she does in a tenement kitchen, to which only an occasional sickly beam of sunlight filters through a grating in the yard; the consequent general dimness of her abode has given her a habit of peering through half-closed eyes. She is slovenly dressed in an old skirt and bodice; her face is grimy, not because her habits are dirty—for, although she is untidy, she is a clean woman—but because of the smoky atmosphere of her room. Her hair is constantly falling over her face, which she is as frequently removing by rapid movements of her right hand). He hasn't turned up yet, an' I'm stiff with the cold waitin' for him.

Seumas. Mr. Grigson, is it?

Mrs. Grigson. Adolphus, Mr. Shields, after takin' his tea at six o'clock—no, I'm tellin' a lie—it was before six, for I remember the Angelus was ringin' out an' we sittin' at the table—after takin' his tea he went out for a breath o' fresh air, an' I haven't seen sign or light of him since. 'Clare to God me heart is up in me mouth, thinkin' he might be shot be the Black an' Tans.

Seumas. Aw, he'll be all right, Mrs. Grigson. You ought to go to bed an' rest yourself; it's always the worst that comes into a body's mind; go to bed, Mrs. Grigson, or you'll catch your death of cold.

Mrs. Grigson. I'm afraid to go to bed, Mr. Shields, for I'm always in dread that some night or another, when he has a sup

taken, he'll fall down the kitchen stairs an' break his neck.
Not that I'd be any the worse if anything did happen to him,
for you know the sort he is, Mr. Shields; sure he has me heart
broke.

Seumas. Don't be downhearted, Mrs. Grigson; he may
take a thought one of these days an' turn over a new leaf.

Mrs. Grigson. Sorra leaf Adolphus 'll ever turn over, he's
too far gone in the horns for that now. Sure no one ud mind
him takin' a pint or two, if he'd stop at that, but he won't;
nothin' could fill him with beer, an' no matter how much he
may have taken, when he's taken more he'll always say,
'Here's the first to-day'.

Davoren (*to Seumas*). Christ! Is she going to stop talking
there all the night?

Seumas. 'Sh, she'll hear you; right enough, the man has
the poor woman's heart broke.

Davoren. And because he has her heart broken, she's to
have the privilege of breaking everybody else's.

Mrs. Grigson. Mr. Shields.

Seumas. Yes?

Mrs. Grigson. Do the insurance companies pay if a man is
shot after curfew?

Seumas. Well, now, that's a thing I couldn't say, Mrs.
Grigson.

Mrs. Grigson (*plaintively*). Isn't he a terrible man to be
takin' such risks, an' not knowin' what'll happen to him?
He knows them Societies only want an excuse to do people out
of their money—is it after one, now, Mr. Shields?

Seumas. Aw, it must be after one, Mrs. Grigson.

Mrs. Grigson (*emphatically*). Ah, then, if I was a young girl
again I'd think twice before gettin' married. Whisht!
There's somebody now—it's him, I know be the way he's
fumblin'.

    [*She goes out a little way. Stumbling steps are heard in the
       hall.*

Mrs. Grigson (outside). Is that you, Dolphie, dear?

[*After a few moments* Adolphus, *with* Mrs. Grigson *holding his arm, stumbles into the room.*

Mrs. Grigson. Dolphie, dear, mind yourself.

Adolphus (he is a man of forty-five, but looks, relatively, much younger than Mrs. Grigson. *His occupation is that of a solicitor's clerk. He has all the appearance of being well fed; and, in fact, he gets most of the nourishment,* Mrs. Grigson *getting just enough to give her strength to do the necessary work of the household. On account of living most of his life out of the kitchen, his complexion is fresh, and his movements, even when sober, are livelier than those of his wife. He is comfortably dressed; heavy top-coat, soft trilby hat, a fancy coloured scarf about his neck, and he carries an umbrella).* I'm all right; do you see anything wrong with me?

Mrs. Grigson. Of course you're all right, dear; there's no one mindin' you.

Adolphus Grigson. Mindin' me, is it, mindin' me? He'd want to be a good thing that ud mind me. There's a man here—a man, mind you, afraid av nothin'—not in this bloody house anyway.

Mrs. Grigson (imploringly). Come on downstairs, Dolphie, dear; sure there's not one in the house ud say a word to you.

Adolphus Grigson. Say a word to me, is it? He'd want to be a good thing that ud say anything to Dolphus Grigson. (*Loudly*) Is there anyone wants to say anything to Dolphus Grigson? If there is, he's here—a man, too—there's no blottin' it out—a man.

Mrs. Grigson. You'll wake everybody in the house; can't you speak quiet?

Adolphus Grigson (more loudly still). What do I care for anybody in the house? Are they keepin' me: are they givin' me anything? When they're keepin' Grigson it'll be time enough for them to talk. (*With a shout*) I can tell them Adolphus Grigson wasn't born in a bottle!

Mrs Grigson (*tearfully*). Why do you talk like that, dear? We all know you weren't born in a bottle.

Adolphus Grigson. There's some of them in this house think Grigson was born in a bottle.

Davoren (*to* Seumas). A most appropriate place for him to be born in.

Mrs. Grigson. Come on down to bed, now, an' you can talk about them in the mornin'.

Grigson. I'll talk about them, now; do you think I'm afraid of them? Dolphus Grigson's afraid av nothin', creepin' or walkin',—if there's any one in the house thinks he's fit to take a fall out av Adolphus Grigson, he's here—a man; they'll find that Grigson's no soft thing.

Davoren. Ah me, alas! Pain, pain ever, for ever.

Mrs. Grigson. Dolphie, dear, poor Mr. Davoren wants to go to bed.

Davoren. Oh, she's terribly anxious about poor Mr. Davoren, all of a sudden.

Grigson (*stumbling towards* Davoren, *and holding out his hand*). Davoren! He's a man. Leave it there, mate. You needn't be afraid av Dolphus Grigson; there never was a drop av informer's blood in the whole family av Grigson. I don't know what you are or what you think, but you're a man, an' not like some of the goughers in this house, that ud hang you. Not referrin' to you, Mr. Shields.

Mrs. Grigson. Oh, you're not deludin' to Mr. Shields.

Seumas. I know that, Mr. Grigson; go on down, now, with Mrs. Grigson, an' have a sleep.

Grigson. I tie myself to no woman's apron-strings, Mr. Shields; I know how to keep Mrs. Grigson in her place; I have the authority of the Bible for that. I know the Bible from cover to cover, Mr. Davoren, an' that's more than some in this house could say. And what does the Holy Scripture say about woman? It says, 'The woman shall be subject to her husband', an' I'll see that Mrs. Grigson keeps the teachin' av the Holy Book in the letter an' in the spirit. If - you're ever in trouble, Mr. Davoren, an' Grigson can help— I'm your man—have you me?

Davoren. I have you, Mr. Grigson, I have you.

Grigson. Right; I'm an Orangeman, an' I'm not ashamed av it, an' I'm not afraid av it, but I can feel for a true man, all the same—have *you* got me, Mr. Shields?

Seumas. Oh, we know you well, Mr. Grigson; many a true Irishman was a Protestant—Tone, Emmet an' Parnell.

Grigson. Mind you, I'm not sayin' as I agree with them you've mentioned, Mr. Shields, for the Bible forbids it, an' Adolphus Grigson 'll always abide be the Bible. Fear God an' honour the King—that's written in Holy Scripture, an' there's no blottin' it out. (*Pulling a bottle out of his pocket.*) But here, Mr. Davoren, have a drink, just to show there's no coolness.

Davoren. No, no, Mr. Grigson, it's late now to take anything. Go on down with Mrs. Grigson, and we can have a chat in the morning.

Grigson. Sure you won't have a drink?

Davoren. Quite sure—thanks all the same.

Grigson (*drinking*). Here's the first to-day! To all true men, even if they were born in a bottle. Here's to King William, to the battle av the Boyne; to the Hobah Black Chapter—that's my Lodge, Mr. Davoren; an' to The Orange Lily O.   [*Singing in a loud shout:*

An' dud ya go to see the show, each rose an' pinkadilly O,
To feast your eyes an' view the prize won be the Orange
    Lily O.
The Vic'roy there, so debonair, just like a daffadilly O,
With Lady Clarke, blithe as a lark, approached the
    Orange Lily O.
       Heigh Ho the Lily O,
       The Royal, Loyal Lily O,

Beneath the sky what flower can vie with Erin's Orange
  Lily O!

Davoren.   Holy God, isn't this terrible!
Grigson (singing):

The elated Muse, to hear the news, jumped like a Connaught
  filly O,
As gossip Fame did loud proclaim the triumph av the
  Lily. O.
The Lowland field may roses yield, gay heaths the High-
  . lands hilly O;
But high or low no flower can show like Erin's Orange
  Lily O.
       Heigh Ho the Lily O,
       The Royal, Loyal Lily O,
Beneath the sky what flower can vie with Erin's Or . . .

> [*While* Grigson *has been singing, the sound of a rapidly
> moving motor is heard, faintly at first, but growing
> rapidly louder, till it apparently stops suddenly somewhere
> very near the house, bringing* Grigson's *song to an abrupt
> conclusion. They are all startled, and listen attentively
> to the throbbing of the engines, which can be plainly heard.*
> Grigson *is considerably sobered, and anxiously keeps
> his eyes on the door.* Seumas *sits up in bed and listens
> anxiously.* Davoren, *with a shaking hand, lights the
> candle, and begins to search hurriedly among the books and
> papers on the table.*

Grigson (with a tremor in his voice).   There's no need to be
afraid, they couldn't be comin' here.

Mrs. Grigson.   God forbid!   It ud be terrible if they came
at this hour ov the night.

Seumas.   You never know now, Mrs. Grigson; they'd
rush in on you when you'd be least expectin' them.   What, in
the name o' God, is goin' to come out of it all?   Nobody now

cares a traneen about the orders of the Ten Commandments; the only order that anybody minds now is, 'Put your hands up'. Oh, it's a hopeless country.

Grigson. Whisht; do you hear them talking outside at the door? You're sure of your life nowhere now; it's just as safe to go everywhere as it is to anywhere. An' they don't give a damn whether you're a loyal man or not. If you're a Republican they make you sing 'God save the King', an' if you're loyal they'll make you sing the 'Soldiers' Song'. The singin' ud be all right if they didn't make you dance afterwards.

Mrs. Grigson. They'd hardly come here unless they heard something about Mr. Davoren.

Davoren. About me! What could they hear about me?

Grigson. You'll never get some people to keep their mouths shut. I was in the Blue Lion this evening, an' who do you think was there, blowin' out av him, but that little blower, Tommy Owens; there he was tellin' everybody that *he* knew where there was bombs; that *he* had a friend that was a General in the I.R.A.; that *he* could tell them what the Staff was thinkin' av doin'; that *he* could lay his hand on tons av revolvers; that they wasn't a mile from where he was livin', but that *he* knew his own know, an' would keep it to himself.

Seumas. Well, God blast the little blower, anyway; it's the like ov him that deserves to be plugged! (*To Davoren*) What are you lookin' for among the books, Donal?

Davoren. A letter that I got to-day from Mr. Gallogher and Mrs. Henderson; I'm blessed if I know where I put it.

Seumas (*peevishly*). Can't you look for it in the mornin'?

Davoren. It's addressed to the Irish Republican Army, and, considering the possibility of a raid, it would be safer to get rid of it.

[*Shots again heard out in the lane, followed by loud shouts of 'Halt, halt, halt!'*

Grigson. I think we had better be gettin' to bed, Debby; it's not right to be keepin' Mr. Davoren an' Mr. Shields awake.

Seumas. An' what made them give you such a letter as that; don't they know the state the country is in? An' you were worse to take it. Have you got it?

Davoren. I can't find it anywhere; isn't this terrible!

Grigson. Good-night, Mr. Davoren; good-night, Mr. Shields.

Mrs. Grigson. Good-night, Mr. Shields; good-night, Mr. Davoren.

> [*They go out.* Seumas *and* Davoren *are too much concerned about the letter to respond to their good-nights.*

Seumas. What were you thinkin' of when you took such a letter as that? Ye gods, has nobody any brains at all, at all? Oh, this is a hopeless country. Did you try in your pockets?

Davoren (*searching in his pockets*). Oh, thanks be to God, here it is.

Seumas. Burn it now, an', for God's sake, don't take any letters like that again. . . . There's the motor goin' away; we can sleep in peace now for the rest of the night. Just to make sure of everything now, have a look in that bag o' Maguire's: not that there can be anything in it.

Davoren. If there's nothing in it, what's the good of looking?

Seumas. It won't kill you to look, will it?

> [*Davoren goes over to the bag, puts it on the table, opens it, and jumps back, his face pale and limbs trembling.*

Davoren. My God, it's full of bombs, Mills bombs!

Seumas. Holy Mother of God, you're jokin'!

Davoren. If the Tans come you'll find whether I'm jokin' or no.

Seumas. Isn't this a nice pickle to be in? St. Anthony, look down on us!

Davoren. There's no use of blaming St. Anthony; why did you let Maguire leave the bag here?

Seumas. Why did I let him leave the bag here; why did I let him leave the bag here! How did I know what was in it?

Didn't I think there was nothin' in it but spoons an' hairpins?
What'll we do now; what'll we do now? Mother o' God,
grant there'll be no raid to-night. I knew things ud go wrong
when I missed Mass this mornin'.

Davoren. Give over your praying and let us try to think
of what is best to be done. There's one thing certain: as
soon as morning comes I'm on the run out of this house.

Seumas. Thinkin' of yourself, like the rest of them. Leavin'
me to bear the brunt of it.

Davoren. And why shouldn't you bear the brunt of it?
Maguire was no friend of mine; besides, it's your fault; you
knew the sort of a man he was, and you should have been on
your guard.

Seumas. Did I know he was a gunman; did I know he was
a gunman, did I know he was a gunman? Did . . .

Davoren. Do you mean to tell me that . . .

Seumas. Just a moment . . .

Davoren. You didn't know . . .

Seumas. Just a moment . . .

Davoren. That Maguire was connected with . . .

Seumas (*loudly*). Just a moment; can't . . .

Davoren. The Republican Movement? What's the use
of trying to tell damn lies!

[*Minnie Powell rushes into the room. She is only partly
dressed, and has thrown a shawl over her shoulders. She is
in a state of intense excitement.*

Minnie. Mr. Davoren, Donal, they're all round the house;
they must be goin' to raid the place; I was lookin' out of the
window an' I seen them; I do be on the watch every night;
have you anything? If you have . . .

[*There is heard at street door a violent and continuous knocking,
followed by the crash of glass and the beating of the door
with rifle-butts.*

Minnie. There they are, there they are, there they are!

[*Davoren reclines almost fainting on the bed; Seumas sits*

*up in an attitude of agonized prayerfulness; Minnie alone
retains her presence of mind. When she sees their panic
she becomes calm, though her words are rapidly · spoken,
and her actions are performed with decisive celerity.*

Minnie.   What is it; what have you got; where are they?

Davoren.   Bombs, bombs, bombs; my God! in the bag
on the table there; we're done, we're done!

Seumas.   Hail, Mary, full of grace—pray for us miserable
sinners—Holy St. Anthony, do you hear them batterin' at the
door—now an' at the hour of our death—say an act of con-
trition, Donal—there's the glass gone!

Minnie.   I'll take them to my room; maybe they won't
search it; if they do aself, they won't harm a girl.   Good-bye
. . . Donal.

> [*She glances lovingly at Donal—who is only semi-conscious—
> as she rushes out with the bag.*

Seumas.   If we come through this I'll never miss a Mass
again! If it's the Tommies it won't be so bad, but if it's the
Tans, we're goin' to have a terrible time.

> [*The street door is broken open and heavy steps are heard in
> the hall, punctuated with shouts of "Old the light 'ere",
> 'Put 'em up', etc. An Auxiliary opens the door of the
> room and enters, revolver in one hand and electric torch in the
> other. His uniform is black, and he wears a black beret.*

The Auxiliary.   'Oo's 'ere?

Seumas (as if he didn't know).   Who—who's that?

The Auxiliary (peremptorily).   'Oo's 'ere?

Seumas.   Only two men, mister; me an' me mate in t'other
bed.

The Auxiliary.   Why didn't you open the door?

Seumas.   We didn't hear you knockin', sir.

The Auxiliary.   You must be a little awd of 'earing, ay?

Seumas.   I had rheumatic fever a few years ago, an' ever
since I do be a—I do be a little deaf sometimes.

The Auxiliary (to Davoren).   'Ow is it you're not in bed?

Davoren. I was in bed; when I heard the knockin' I got up to open the door.

The Auxiliary. *You're* a koind blowke, you are. Deloighted, like, to have a visit from us, ay? Ah? (*Threatening to strike him*) Why down't you answer?

Davoren. Yes, sir.

The Auxiliary. What's your name?

Davoren. Davoren, Dan Davoren, sir.

The Auxiliary. You're not an Irishman, are you?

Davoren. I-I-I was born in Ireland.

The Auxiliary. Ow, you were, were you; Irish han' proud of it, ay? (*To Seumas*) What's *your* name?

Seumas. Seuma . . . Oh no; Jimmie Shields, sir.

The Auxiliary. Ow, you're a selt (*he means a Celt*), one of the seltic race that speaks a lingo of its ahn, and that's going to overthrow the British Empire—I don't think! 'Ere, where's your gun?

Seumas. I never had a gun in me hand in me life.

The Auxiliary. Now; you wouldn't know what a gun is if you sawr one, I suppowse. (*Displaying his revolver in a careless way*) 'Ere, what's that?

Seumas. Oh, be careful, please, be careful.

The Auxiliary. Why, what 'ave I got to be careful abaht?

Seumas. The gun; it-it-it might go off.

The Auxiliary. An' what prawse if it did; it can easily be relowded. Any ammunition 'ere? What's in that press?

           [*He searches and scatters contents of press.*

Seumas. Only a little bit o' grub; you'll get nothin' here, sir; no one in the house has any connection with politics.

The Auxiliary. Now? I've never met a man yet that didn't say that, but we're a little bit too ikey now to be kidded with that sort of talk.

Seumas. May I go an' get a drink o' water?

The Auxiliary. You'll want a barrel of watah before you're done with us. (*The Auxiliary goes about the room examining places*) 'Ello, what's 'ere? A statue o' Christ! An' a Cruci-fix! You'd think you was in a bloomin' monastery.

[*Mrs. Grigson enters, dressed disorderly and her hair awry.*

Mrs. Grigson. They're turning the place upside-down Upstairs an' downstairs they're makin' a litter of everything! I declare to God, it's awful what law-abidin' people have to put up with. An' they found a pint bottle of whisky under Dolphie's pillow, an' they're drinkin' every drop of it—an' Dolphie'll be like a devil in the mornin' when he finds he has no curer.

The Auxiliary (*all attention when he hears the word whisky*). A bottle of whisky, ay? 'Ere, where do you live—quick, where do you live?

Mrs. Grigson. Down in the kitchen—an' when you go down will you ask them not to drink—oh, he's gone without listenin' to me.

[*While* Mrs. Grigson *is speaking the* Auxiliary *rushes out.*

Seumas (*anxiously to* Mrs. Grigson). Are they searchin' the whole house, Mrs. Grigson?

Mrs. Grigson. They didn't leave a thing in the kitchen that they didn't flitter about the floor; the things in the cup-board, all the little odds an' ends that I keep in the big box, an . . .

Seumas. Oh, they're a terrible gang of blaguards—did they go upstairs?—they'd hardly search Minnie Powell's room—do you think, would they, Mrs. Grigson?

Mrs. Grigson. Just to show them the sort of a man he was, before they come in, Dolphie put the big Bible on the table, open at the First Gospel of St. Peter, second chapter, an' marked the thirteenth to the seventeenth verse in red ink—you know the passages, Mr. Shields—(*quoting*):

'Submit yourselves to every ordinance of man for the Lord's sake: whether it be to the king, as supreme; or unto governors, as unto them that are sent by him for the punish-

ment of evildoers, an' for the praise of them that do well.
. . . Love the brotherhood. Fear God. Honour the
King.'

An' what do you think they did, Mr. Shields? They caught
a hold of the Bible an' flung it on the floor—imagine that,
Mr. Shields—flingin' the Bible on the floor! Then one of
them says to another—'Jack,' says he, 'have you seen the
light; is your soul saved?' An' then they grabbed hold of
poor Dolphie, callin' him Mr. Moody an' Mr. Sankey, an'
wanted him to offer up a prayer for the Irish Republic! An'
when they were puttin' me out, there they had the poor man
sittin' up in bed, his hands crossed on his breast, his eyes
lookin' up at the ceilin', an' he singin' a hymn—'We shall
meet in the Sweet Bye an' Bye'—an' all the time, Mr. Shields,
there they were drinkin' his whisky; there's torture for you,
an' they all laughin' at poor Dolphie's terrible sufferin's.

   Davoren. In the name of all that's sensible, what did he
want to bring whisky home with him for? They're bad
enough sober, what'll they be like when they're drunk?

   Mrs. Grigson (plaintively). He always brings a drop home
with him—he calls it his medicine.

   Seumas (still anxious). They'll hardly search all the house;
do you think they will, Mrs. Grigson?

   Mrs. Grigson. An' we have a picture over the mantelpiece
of King William crossing the Boyne, an' do you know what
they wanted to make out, Mr. Shields, that it was Robert
Emmet, an' the picture of a sacret society!

   Seumas. She's not listenin' to a word I'm sayin'! Oh,
the country is hopeless an' the people is hopeless.

   Davoren. For God's sake tell her to go to hell out of this—
she's worse than the Auxsie.

   Seumas (thoughtfully). Let her stay where she is; it's safer
to have a woman in the room. If they come across the bombs
I hope to God Minnie'll say nothin'.

Davoren. We're a pair of pitiable cowards to let poor Minnie suffer when we know that we and not she are to blame.

Seumas. What else can we do, man? Do you want us to be done in? If you're anxious to be riddled, I'm not. Besides, they won't harm her, she's only a girl, an' so long as she keeps her mouth shut it'll be all right.

Davoren. I wish I could be sure of that.

Seumas. D'ye think are they goin', Mrs. Grigson? What are they doin' now?

Mrs. Grigson (who is standing at the door, looking out into the hall). There's not a bit of me that's not shakin' like a jelly!

Seumas. Are they gone upstairs, Mrs. Grigson? Do you think, Mrs. Grigson, will they soon be goin'?

Mrs. Grigson. When they were makin' poor Dolphie sit up in the bed, I 'clare to God I thought every minute I'd hear their guns goin' off, an' see poor Dolphie stretched out dead in the bed—whisht, God bless us, I think I hear him moanin'!

Seumas. You might as well be talking to a stone! They're all hopeless, hopeless, hopeless! She thinks she hears him moanin'! It's bloody near time somebody made him moan!

Davoren (with a sickly attempt at humour). He's moaning for the loss of his whisky.

> [*During the foregoing dialogue the various sounds of a raid —orders, the tramping of heavy feet, the pulling about of furniture, etc.—are heard. Now a more definite and sustained commotion is apparent. Loud and angry commands of 'Go on', 'Get out and get into the lorry', are heard, mingled with a girl's voice—it is Minnie's—shouting bravely, but a little hysterically, 'Up the Republic'.*]

Mrs. Grigson (from the door). God save us, they're takin' Minnie, they're takin' Minnie Powell! (*Running out*) What in the name of God can have happened?

Seumas. Holy Saint Anthony grant that she'll keep her mouth shut.

Davoren (sitting down on the bed and covering his face with his hands). We'll never again be able to lift up our heads if anything happens to Minnie.

Seumas. For God's sake keep quiet or somebody'll hear you; nothin'll happen to her, nothin' at all—it'll be all right if she only keeps her mouth shut.

Mrs. Grigson (*running in*). They're after gettin' a whole lot of stuff in Minnie's room! Enough to blow up the whole street, a Tan says! God to-night, who'd have ever thought that of Minnie Powell!

Seumas. Did she say anything, is she sayin' anything, what's she sayin', Mrs. Grigson?

Mrs. Grigson. She's shoutin' 'Up the Republic' at the top of her voice. An' big Mrs. Henderson is fightin' with the soldiers—she's after nearly knockin' one of them down, an' they're puttin' her into the lorry too.

Seumas. God blast her! Can she not mind her own business? What does she want here—didn't she know there was a raid on? Is the whole damn country goin' mad? They'll open fire in a minute an' innocent people'll be shot!

Davoren. What way are they using Minnie, Mrs. Grigson; are they rough with her?

Mrs. Grigson. They couldn't be half rough enough; the little hussy, to be so deceitful; she might as well have had the house blew up! God to-night, who'd think it was in Minnie Powell!

Seumas. Oh, grant she won't say anything!

Mrs. Grigson. There they're goin' away now; ah, then I hope they'll give that Minnie Powell a coolin'.

Seumas. God grant she won't say anything! Are they gone, Mrs. Grigson?

Mrs. Grigson. With her fancy stockin's, an' her pompoms, an' her crepe de chine blouses! I knew she'd come to no good!

Seumas. God grant she'll keep her mouth shut! Are they gone, Mrs. Grigson?

Mrs. Grigson. They're gone, Mr. Shields, an' here's poor Dolphie an' not a feather astray on him. Oh, Dolphie, dear, you're all right, thanks to God; I thought you'd never see the mornin'.

Grigson (*entering without coat or vest*). Of course I'm all right; what ud put a bother on Dolphie Grigson?—not the Tans anyway!

Mrs. Grigson. When I seen you stretched out on the bed, an' you . . . singin' a hymn . . .

Grigson (*fearful of possible humiliation*). Who was singin' a hymn? D'ye hear me talkin' to you—where did you hear me singin' a hymn?

Mrs. Grigson. I was only jokin', Dolphie, dear; I . . .

Grigson. Your place is below, an' not gosterin' here to men; down with you quick!

[*Mrs. Grigson hurriedly leaves the room.*

Grigson (*nonchalantly taking out his pipe, filling it, lighting it, and beginning to smoke*). Excitin' few moments, Mr. Davoren; Mrs. G. lost her head completely—panic-stricken. But that's only natural, all women is very nervous. The only thing to do is to show them that they can't put the wind up you; show the least sign of fright an' they'd walk on you, simply walk on you. Two of them come down—'Put them up', revolvers under your nose—you know, the usual way. 'What's all the bother about?' says I, quite calm. 'No bother at all,' says one of them, 'only this gun might go off an' hit somebody— have you me?' says he. 'What if it does,' says I; 'a man can only die once, an' you'll find Grigson won't squeal.' 'God, you're a cool one,' says the other, 'there's no blottin' it out.'

Seumas. That's the best way to take them; it only makes things worse to show that you've got the wind up. 'Any ammunition here?' says the fellow that come in here. 'I don't think so,' says I, 'but you better have a look.' 'No back talk,' says he, 'or you might get plugged.' 'I don't know of any clause,' says I, 'in the British Constitution that makes it a crime for a man to speak in his own room,'—with that, he just had a look round, an' off he went.

Grigson. If a man keeps a stiff upper front—Merciful God, there's an ambush!

> [*Explosions of two bursting bombs are heard on the street outside the house, followed by fierce and rapid revolver fire. People are heard rushing into the hall, and there is general clamour and confusion. Seumas and Davoren cower down in the room; Grigson, after a few moments' hesitation, frankly rushes out of the room to what he conceives to be the safer asylum of the kitchen. A lull follows, punctured by an odd rifle-shot; then comes a peculiar and ominous stillness, broken in a few moments by the sounds of voices and movement. Questions are heard being asked: 'Who was it was killed?' 'Where was she shot?' which are answered by: 'Minnie Powell'; 'She went to jump off the lorry an' she was shot'; 'She's not dead, is she?'; 'They say she's dead —shot through the buzzom!'*

Davoren (*in a tone of horror-stricken doubt*). D'ye hear what they're sayin', Shields, dy'e hear what they're sayin'—Minnie Powell is shot.

Seumas. For God's sake speak easy, an' don't bring them in here on top of us again.

Davoren. Is that all you're thinking of? Do you realize that she has been shot to save us?

Seumas. Is it my fault; am I to blame?

Davoren. It is your fault and mine, both; oh, we're a pair of dastardly cowards to have let her do what she did.

Seumas. She did it off her own bat—we didn't ask her to do it.

> [Mrs. Grigson *enters. She is excited and semi-hysterical, and sincerely affected by the tragic occurrence.*

Mrs. Grigson (*falling down in a sitting posture on one of the beds*). What's goin' to happen next! Oh, Mr. Davoren, isn't it terrible, isn't it terrible! Minnie Powell, poor little Minnie

Powell's been shot dead! They were raidin' a house a few doors down, an' had just got up in their lorries to go away, when they was ambushed. You never heard such shootin'! An' in the thick of it, poor Minnie went to jump off the lorry she was on, an' she was shot through the buzzom. Oh, it was horrible to see the blood pourin' out, an' Minnie moanin'. They found some paper in her breast, with 'Minnie' written on it, an' some other name they couldn't make out with the blood; the officer kep' it. The ambulance is bringin' her to the hospital, but what good's that when she's dead! Poor little Minnie, poor little Minnie Powell, to think of you full of a life a few minutes ago, an' now she's dead!

Davoren. Ah me, alas! Pain, pain, pain ever, for ever! It's terrible to think that little Minnie is dead, but it's still more terrible to think that Davoren and Shields are alive! Oh, Donal Davoren, shame is your portion now till the silver cord is loosened and the golden bowl be broken. Oh, Davoren, Donal Davoren, poet and poltroon, poltroon and poet!

Seumas (solemnly). I knew something ud come of the tappin' on the wall!

CURTAIN

THE PLOUGH AND THE STARS

A Tragedy in Four Acts

TO THE GAY LAUGH OF MY MOTHER
AT THE GATE OF THE GRAVE

CHARACTERS IN THE PLAY

JACK CLITHEROE (*a bricklayer*), *Commandant in the Irish Citizen Army*
NORA CLITHEROE, *his wife*
PETER FLYNN (*a labourer*), *Nora's uncle*
THE YOUNG COVEY (*a fitter*), *Clitheroe's cousin* } *Residents in the Tenement*
BESSIE BURGESS (*a street fruit-vendor*)
MRS. GOGAN (*a charwoman*)
MOLLSER, *her consumptive child*
FLUTHER GOOD (*a carpenter*)
LIEUT. LANGON (*a Civil Servant*), *of the Irish Volunteers*
CAPT. BRENNAN (*a chicken butcher*), *of the Irish Citizen Army*
CORPORAL STODDART, *of the Wiltshires*
SERGEANT TINLEY, *of the Wiltshires*
ROSIE REDMOND, *a daughter of 'the Digs'*
A BAR-TENDER
A WOMAN
THE FIGURE IN THE WINDOW

———

ACT I.—The living-room of the Clitheroe flat in a Dublin tenement.
ACT II.—A public-house, outside of which a meeting is being held.
ACT III.—The street outside the Clitheroe tenement.
ACT IV.—The room of Bessie Burgess.

———

TIME.—ACTS I and II, November 1915; Acts III and IV, Easter Week, 1916. A few days elapse between Acts III and IV.

ACT I

The home of the Clitheroes. *It consists of the front and back drawing-rooms in a fine old Georgian house, struggling for its life against the assaults of time, and the more savage assaults of the tenants. The room shown is the back drawing-room, wide, spacious, and lofty. At back is the entrance to the front drawing-room. The space, originally occupied by folding doors, is now draped with casement cloth of a dark purple, decorated with a design in reddish-purple and cream. One of the curtains is pulled aside, giving a glimpse of front drawing-room, at the end of which can be seen the wide, lofty windows looking out into the street. The room directly in front of the audience is furnished in a way that suggests an attempt towards a finer expression of domestic life. The large fireplace on right is of wood, painted to look like marble (the original has been taken away by the landlord). On the mantelshelf are two candlesticks of dark carved wood. Between them is a small clock. Over the clock is hanging a calendar which displays a picture of 'The Sleeping Venus'. In the centre of the breast of the chimney hangs a picture of Robert Emmet. On the right of the entrance to the front drawing-room is a copy of 'The Gleaners', on the opposite side a copy of 'The Angelus'. Underneath 'The Gleaners' is a chest of drawers on which stands a green bowl filled with scarlet dahlias and white chrysanthemums. Near to the fireplace is a settee which at night forms a double bed for* Clitheroe *and* Nora. *Underneath 'The Angelus' are a number of shelves containing saucepans and a frying-pan. Under these is a table on which are various articles of delf ware. Near the end of the room, opposite to the fireplace, is a gate-legged table, covered with a cloth. On top of the table a huge cavalry sword is lying. To the right is a door which leads to a lobby from which the staircase leads to the hall. The floor is covered with a dark green linoleum. The room is dim except where it is illuminated*

135

from the glow of the fire. Through the window of the room at back can be seen the flaring of the flame of a gasolene lamp giving light to workmen repairing the street. Occasionally can be heard the clang of crowbars striking the setts. Fluther Good *is repairing the lock of door, Right. A claw-hammer is on a chair beside him, and he has a screw-driver in his hand. He is a man of forty years of age, rarely surrendering to thoughts of anxiety, fond of his 'oil' but determined to conquer the habit before he dies. He is square-jawed and harshly featured; under the left eye is a scar, and his nose is bent from a smashing blow received in a fistic battle long ago. He is bald, save for a few peeping tufts of reddish hair around his ears; and his upper lip is hidden by a scrubby red moustache, embroidered here and there with a grey hair. He is dressed in a seedy black suit, cotton shirt with a soft collar, and wears a very respectable little black bow. On his head is a faded jerry hat, which, when he is excited, he has a habit of knocking farther back on his head, in a series of taps. In an argument he usually fills with sound and fury generally signifying a row. He is in his shirt-sleeves at present, and wears a soiled white apron, from a pocket in which sticks a carpenter's two-foot rule. He has just finished the job of putting on a new lock, and, filled with satisfaction, he is opening and shutting the door, enjoying the completion of a work well done. Sitting at the fire, airing a white shirt, is* Peter Flynn. *He is a little, thin bit of a man, with a face shaped like a lozenge; on his cheeks and under his chin is a straggling wiry beard of a dirty-white and lemon hue. His face invariably wears a look of animated anguish, mixed with irritated defiance, as if everybody was at war with him, and he at war with everybody. He is cocking his head in a way that suggests resentment at the presence of* Fluther, *who pays no attention to him, apparently, but is really furtively watching him.* Peter *is clad in a singlet, white whipcord knee-breeches, and is in his stocking-feet.*

A voice is heard speaking outside of door, Left (it is that of Mrs. Gogan).

Mrs. Gogan *(outside)*. Who are you lookin' for, sir? Who?

Mrs. Clitheroe? . . . Oh, excuse me. Oh ay, up this way.
She's out, I think: I seen her goin'. Oh, you've somethin'
for her; oh, excuse me. You're from Arnott's. . . . I see. . . .
You've a parcel for her. . . . Righto. . . . I'll take it. . . . I'll
give it to her the minute she comes in. . . . It'll be quite safe.
. . . Oh, sign that. . . . Excuse me. . . . Where? . . . Here?
. . . No, there; righto. Am I to put Maggie or Mrs.?
What is it? You dunno? Oh, excuse me.

> [Mrs. Gogan *opens the door and comes in. She is a doleful-
> looking little woman of forty, insinuating manner and
> sallow complexion. She is fidgety and nervous, terribly
> talkative, has a habit of taking up things that may be
> near her and fiddling with them while she is speaking. Her
> heart is aflame with curiosity, and a fly could not come
> into nor go out of the house without her knowing. She
> has a draper's parcel in her hand, the knot of the twine
> tying it is untied.* Peter, *more resentful of this intrusion
> than of* Fluther's *presence, gets up from the chair, and
> without looking around, his head carried at an angry
> cock, marches into the room at back.*

Mrs. Gogan (*removing the paper and opening the cardboard box
it contains*). I wondher what's this now? A hat! (*She
takes out a hat, black, with decorations in red and gold.*) God,
she's goin' to th' divil lately for style! That hat, now, cost
more than a penny. Such notions of upperosity she's gettin'.
(*Putting the hat on her head*) Oh, swank, what!

> [*She replaces it in parcel.*

Fluther. She's a pretty little Judy, all the same.

Mrs. Gogan. Ah, she is, an' she isn't. There's prettiness
an' prettiness in it. I'm always sayin' that her skirts are a
little too short for a married woman. An' to see her, sometimes of an evenin', in her glad-neck gown would make a
body's blood run cold. I do be ashamed of me life before
her husband. An' th' way she thries to be polite, with her
'Good mornin', Mrs. Gogan', when she's goin' down, an' her

'Good evenin', Mrs. Gogan', when she's comin' up. But there's politeness an' politeness in it.

Fluther. They seem to get on well together, all th' same.

Mrs. Gogan. Ah, they do, an' they don't. The pair o' them used to be like two turtle doves always billin' an' cooin'. You couldn't come into th' room but you'd feel, instinctive like, that they'd just been afther kissin' an' cuddlin' each other. . . . It often made me shiver, for, afther all, there's kissin' an' cuddlin' in it. But I'm thinkin' he's beginnin' to take things more quietly; the mysthery of havin' a woman's a mysthery no longer. . . . She dhresses herself to keep him with her, but it's no use—afther a month or two, th' wondher of a woman wears off.

Fluther. I dunno, I dunno. Not wishin' to say anything derogatory, I think it's all a question of location : when a man finds th' wondher of one woman beginnin' to die, it's usually beginnin' to live in another.

Mrs. Gogan. She's always grumblin' about havin' to live in a tenement house. 'I wouldn't like to spend me last hour in one, let alone live me life in a tenement,' says she. 'Vaults,' says she, 'that are hidin' th' dead, instead of homes that are sheltherin' th' livin'.' 'Many a good one,' says I, 'was reared in a tenement house.' Oh, you know, she's a well-up little lassie, too; able to make a shillin' go where another would have to spend a pound. She's wipin' th' eyes of th' Covey an' poor oul' Pether—everybody knows that—screwin' every penny she can out o' them, in ordher to turn th' place into a babby-house. An' she has th' life frightened out o' them; washin' their face, combin' their hair, wipin' their feet, brushin' their clothes, thrimmin' their nails, cleanin' their teeth—God Almighty, you'd think th' poor men were undhergoin' penal servitude.

Fluther (*with an exclamation of disgust*). A-a-ah, that's goin' beyond th' beyonds in a tenement house. That's a little bit too derogatory.

[*Peter enters from room, Back, head elevated and resentful fire in his eyes; he is still in his singlet and trousers, but is now wearing a pair of unlaced boots—possibly to be decent in the presence of Mrs. Gogan. He places the white shirt, which he has carried in on his arm, on the back of a chair near the fire, and, going over to the chest of drawers, he opens drawer after drawer, looking for something; as he fails to find it he closes each drawer with a snap; he pulls out pieces of linen neatly folded, and bundles them back again any way.*

Peter (*in accents of anguish*). Well, God Almighty, give me patience!

[*He returns to room, Back, giving the shirt a vicious turn as he passes.*

Mrs. Gogan. I wondher what he is foostherin' for now?

Fluther. He's adornin' himself for th' meeting to-night. (*Pulling a handbill from his pocket and reading*) 'Great Demonstration an' torchlight procession around places in th' city sacred to th' memory of Irish Patriots, to be concluded be a meetin', at which will be taken an oath of fealty to th' Irish Republic. Formation in Parnell Square at eight o'clock.' Well, they can hold it for Fluther. I'm up th' pole; no more dhrink for Fluther. It's three days now since I touched a dhrop, an' I feel a new man already.

Mrs. Gogan. Isn't oul' Peter a funny-lookin' little man? . . . Like somethin' you'd pick off a Christmas Tree. . . . When he's dhressed up in his canonicals, you'd wondher where he'd been got. God forgive me, when I see him in them, I always think he must ha' had a Mormon for a father! He an' th' Covey can't abide each other; the' pair o' them is always at it, thryin' to best each other. There'll be blood dhrawn one o' these days.

Fluther. How is it that Clitheroe himself, now, doesn't have anythin' to do with th' Citizen Army? A couple o'

months ago, an' you'd hardly ever see him without his gun,
an' th' Red Hand o' Liberty Hall in his hat.

Mrs. Gogan. Just because he wasn't made a Captain of.
He wasn't goin' to be in anything where he couldn't be
conspishuous. He was so cocksure o' being made one that
he bought a Sam Browne belt, an' was always puttin' it on an'
standin' at th' door showing it off, till th' man came an' put
out th' street lamps on him. God, I think he used to bring it
to bed with him! But I'm tellin' you herself was delighted
that that cock didn't crow, for she's like a clockin' hen if he
leaves her sight for a minute.

[*While she is talking, she takes up book after book from the
table, looks into each of them in a near-sighted way, and
then leaves them back. She now lifts up the sword, and
proceeds to examine it.*

Mrs. Gogan. Be th' look of it, this must ha' been a general's
sword. . . . All th' gold lace an' th' fine figaries on it. . . .
Sure it's twiced too big for him.

Fluther. A-ah; it's a baby's rattle he ought to have, an'
he as he is with thoughts tossin' in his head of what may happen
to him on th' day o' judgement.

[*Peter has entered, and seeing* Mrs. Gogan *with the sword,
goes over to her, pulls it resentfully out of her hands, and
marches into the room, Back, without speaking.*

Mrs. Gogan (*as* Peter *whips the sword*). Oh, excuse me! . . .
(*To* Fluther) Isn't he th' surly oul' rascal!

Fluther. Take no notice of him. . . . You'd think he was
dumb, but when you get his goat, or he has a few jars up, he's
vice versa.   [*He coughs.*

Mrs. Gogan (*she has now sidled over as far as the shirt hanging on
the chair*). Oh, you've got a cold on you, Fluther.

Fluther (*carelessly*). Ah, it's only a little one.

Mrs. Gogan. You'd want to be careful, all th' same. I
knew a woman, a big lump of a woman, red-faced an' round-
bodied, a little awkward on her feet; you'd think, to look at

her, she could put out her two arms an' lift a two-storied house on th' top of her head; got a ticklin' in her throat, an' a little cough, an' th' next mornin' she had a little catchin' in her chest, an' they had just time to wet her lips with a little rum, an' off she went.   [*She begins to look at and handle the shirt.*

Fluther (a little nervously). It's only a little cold I have; there's nothing derogatory wrong with me.

Mrs. Gogan. I dunno; there's many a man this minute lowerin' a pint, thinkin' of a woman, or pickin' out a winner, or doin' work as you're doin', while th' hearse dhrawn be th' horses with the black plumes is dhrivin' up to his own hall door, an' a voice that he doesn't hear is muttherin' in his ear, 'Earth to earth, an' ashes t' ashes, an' dust to dust.'

Fluther (faintly). A man in th' pink o' health should have a holy horror of allowin' thoughts o' death to be festerin' in his mind, for (*with a frightened cough*) be God, I think I'm afther gettin' a little catch in me chest that time—it's a creepy thing to be thinkin' about.

Mrs. Gogan. It is, an' it isn't; it's both bad an' good. . . . It always gives meself a kind o' threspassin' joy to feel meself movin' along in a mournin' coach, an' me thinkin' that, maybe, th' next funeral 'll be me own, an' glad, in a quiet way, that this is somebody else's.

Fluther. An' a curious kind of a gaspin' for breath—I hope there's nothin' derogatory wrong with me.

Mrs. Gogan (examining the shirt). Frills on it, like a woman's petticoat.

Fluther. Suddenly gettin' hot, an' then, just as suddenly, gettin' cold.

Mrs. Gogan (holding out the shirt towards Fluther). How would you like to be wearin' this Lord Mayor's nightdhress, Fluther?

Fluther (vehemently). Blast you an' your nightshirt! Is a man fermentin' with fear to stick th' showin' off to him of a thing that looks like a shinin' shroud?

Mrs. Gogan. Oh, excuse me!

[*Peter has again entered, and he pulls the shirt from the hands of Mrs. Gogan, replacing it on the chair. He returns to room.*

Peter (as he goes out). Well, God Almighty, give me patience!

Mrs. Gogan (to Peter). Oh, excuse me!

[*There is heard a cheer from the men working outside on the street, followed by the clang of tools being thrown down, then silence. The glare of the gasolene light diminishes and finally goes out.*

Mrs. Gogan (running into the back room to look out of the window]. What's the men repairin' th' streets cheerin' for?

Fluther (sitting down weakly on a chair). You can't sneeze but that oul' one wants to know th' why an' th' wherefore. . . . I feel as dizzy as bedamned! I hope I didn't give up th' beer too suddenly.

[*The* Covey *comes in by the door, Right. He is about twenty-five, tall, thin, with lines on his face that form a perpetual protest against life as he conceives it to be. Heavy seams fall from each side of nose, down around his lips, as if they were suspenders keeping his mouth from falling. He speaks in a slow, wailing drawl; more rapidly when he is excited. He is dressed in dungarees, and is wearing a vividly red tie. He flings his cap with a gesture of disgust on the table, and begins to take off his overalls.*

Mrs. Gogan (to the Covey, *as she runs back into the room).* What's after happenin', Covey?

The Covey (with contempt). Th' job's stopped. They've been mobilized to march in th' demonstration to-night undher th' Plough an' th' Stars. Didn't you hear them cheerin', th' mugs! They have to renew their political baptismal vows to be faithful in seculo seculorum.

Fluther (forgetting his fear in his indignation). There's no reason to bring religion into it. I think we ought to have as great a regard for religion as we can, so as to keep it out of as many things as possible.

The Covey (*pausing in the taking off of his dungarees*). Oh, you're one o' the boys that climb into religion as high as a short Mass on Sunday mornin's? I suppose you'll be singin' songs o' Sion an' songs o' Tara at th' meetin', too.

Fluther. We're all Irishmen, anyhow; aren't we?

The Covey (*with hand outstretched, and in a professional tone*). Look here, comrade, there's no such thing as an Irishman, or an Englishman, or a German or a Turk; we're all only human bein's. Scientifically speakin', it's all a question of the accidental gatherin' together of mollycewels an' atoms.

[*Peter comes in with a collar in his hand. He goes over to mirror, Left, and proceeds to try to put it on.*

Fluther. Mollycewels an' atoms! D'ye think I'm goin' to listen to you thryin' to juggle Fluther's mind with complicated cunundhrums of mollycewels an' atoms?

The Covey (*rather loudly*). There's nothin' complicated in it. There's no fear o' the Church tellin' you that mollycewels is a stickin' together of millions of atoms o' sodium, carbon, potassium o' iodide, etcetera, that, accordin' to th' way they're mixed, make a flower, a fish, a star that you see shinin' in th' sky, or a man with a big brain like me, or a man with a little brain like you!

Fluther (*more loudly still*). There's no necessity to be raisin' your voice; shoutin's no manifestin' forth of a growin' mind.

Peter (*struggling with his collar*). God, give me patience with this thing. . . . She makes these collars as stiff with starch as a shinin' band o' solid steel! She does it purposely to thry an' twart me. If I can't get it on th' singlet, how, in th' Name o' God, am I goin' to get it on th' shirt?

The Covey (*loudly*). There's no use o' arguin' with you; it's education you want, comrade.

Fluther. The Covey an' God made th' world, I suppose, wha'?

The Covey. When I hear some men talkin' I'm inclined to disbelieve that th' world's eight-hundhred million years old, for it's not long since th' fathers o' some o' them crawled out o' th' sheltherin' slime o' the sea.

Mrs. Gogan (from room at back). There, they're afther formin' fours, an' now they're goin' to march away.

Fluther (scornfully). Mollycewels! (*He begins to untie his apron.*) What about Adam an' Eve?

The Covey. Well, what about them?

Fluther (fiercely). What about them, you?

The Covey. Adam an' Eve! Is that as far as you've got? Are you still thinkin' there was nobody in th' world before Adam and Eve? (*Loudly*) Did you ever hear, man, of th' skeleton of th' man o' Java?

Peter (casting the collar from him). Blast it, blast it, blast it !

Fluther (viciously folding his apron). Ah, you're not goin' to be let tap your rubbidge o' thoughts into th' mind o' Fluther.

The Covey. You're afraid to listen to th' thruth!

Fluther. Who's afraid?

The Covey. You are!

Fluther. G'way, you wurum!

The Covey. Who's a worum?

Fluther. You are, or you wouldn't talk th' way you're talkin'.

The Covey. Th' oul', ignorant savage leppin' up in you, when science shows you that th' head of your god is an empty one. Well, I hope you're enjoyin' th' blessin' o' havin' to live be th' sweat of your brow.

Fluther. You'll be kickin' an' yellin' for th' priest yet, me boyo. I'm not goin' to stand silent an' simple listenin' to a thick like you makin' a maddenin' mockery o' God Almighty. It 'ud be a nice derogatory thing on me conscience, an' me dyin', to look back in rememberin' shame of talkin' to a word-weavin' little ignorant yahoo of a red flag Socialist !

Mrs. Gogan (she has returned to the front room, and has wandered around looking at things in general, and is now in front of the fireplace looking at the picture hanging over it). For God's sake, Fluther, dhrop it; there's always th' makin's of a row in th' mention of religion . . . *(Looking at picture)* God bless us, it's a naked woman!

Fluther (coming over to look at it). What's undher it? *(Reading)* 'Georgina: The Sleepin' Vennis'. Oh, that's a terrible picture; oh, that's a shockin' picture! Oh, th' one that got that taken, she must have been a prime lassie!

Peter (who also has come over to look, laughing, with his body bent at the waist, and his head slighly tilted back). Hee, hee, hee, hee, hee!

Fluther (indignantly, to Peter). What are you hee, hee-in' for? That' a nice thing to be hee, hee-in' at. Where's your morality, man?

Mrs. Gogan. God forgive us, it's not right to be lookin' at it.

Fluther. It's nearly a derogatory thing to be in th' room where it is.

Mrs. Gogan (giggling hysterically). I couldn't stop any longer in th' same room with three men, afther lookin' at it!

[*She goes out.*

[*The* Covey, *who has divested himself of his dungaress, throws them with a contemptuous motion on top of* Peter's *white shirt.*

Peter (plaintively). Where are you throwin' them? Are you thryin' to twart an' torment me again?

The Covey. Who's thryin' to twart you?

Peter (flinging the dungarees violently on the floor). You're not goin' to make me lose me temper, me young Covey.

The Covey (flinging the white shirt on the floor). If you're Nora's pet, aself, you're not goin' to get your way in everything.

Peter (plaintively, with his eyes looking up at the ceiling). I'll say nothin'. . . . I'll leave you to th' day when th' all-pitiful, all-merciful, all-lovin' God 'll be handin' you to th' angels to be rievin' an' roastin' you, tearin' an' tormentin' you, burnin' an' blastin' you!

The Covey. Aren't you th' little malignant oul' bastard, you lemon-whiskered oul' swine!

[*Peter runs to the sword, draws it, and makes for the* Covey, *who dodges him around the table; Peter has no intention of striking, but the* Covey *wants to take no chance.*

The Covey (*dodging*). Fluther, hold him, there. It's a nice thing to have a lunatic like this lashin' around with a lethal weapon!

[*The* Covey *darts out of the room, Right, slamming the door in the face of* Peter.

Peter (*battering and pulling at the door*). Lemme out, lemme out; isn't it a poor thing for a man who wouldn't say a word against his greatest enemy to have to listen to that Covey's twartin' animosities, shovin' poor, patient people into a lashin' out of curses that darken his soul with th' shadow of th' wrath of th' last day!

Fluther. Why d'ye take notice of him? If he seen you didn't, he'd say nothin' derogatory.

Peter. I'll make him stop his laughin' an' leerin', jibin' an' jeerin' an' scarifyin' people with his corner-boy insinuations! . . . He's always thryin' to rouse me: if it's not a song, it's a whistle; if it isn't a whistle, it's a cough. But you can taunt an' taunt—I'm laughin' at you; he, hee, hee, hee, hee, heee!

The Covey (*singing through the keyhole*):

Dear harp o' me counthry, in darkness I found thee,
The dark chain of silence had hung o'er thee long—

Peter (*frantically*). Jasus, d'ye hear that? D'ye hear him soundin' forth his divil-souled song o' provocation?

The Covey (*singing as before*):

When proudly, me own island harp, I unbound thee,
An' gave all thy chords to light, freedom an' song!

Peter (battering at door). When I get out I'll do for you, I'll do for you, I'll do for you!

The Covey (through the keyhole). Cuckoo-oo!

[*Nora enters by door, Right. She is a young woman of twenty-two, alert, swift, full of nervous energy, and a little anxious to get on in the world. The firm lines of her face are considerably opposed by a soft, amorous mouth and gentle eyes. When her firmness fails her, she persuades with her feminine charm. She is dressed in a tailor-made costume, and wears around her neck a silver fox fur.*

Nora (running in and pushing Peter away from the door). Oh, can I not turn me back but th' two o' yous are at it like a pair o' fightin' cocks! Uncle Peter . . . Uncle Peter . . . UNCLE PETER!

Peter (vociferously). Oh, Uncle Peter, Uncle Peter be damned! D'ye think I'm goin' to give a free pass to th' young Covey to turn me whole life into a Holy Manual o' penances an' martyrdoms?

The Covey (angrily rushing into the room). If you won't exercise some sort o' conthrol over that Uncle Peter o' yours, there'll be a funeral, an' it won't be me that'll be in th' hearse!

Nora (between Peter and the Covey, to the Covey). Are yous always goin' to be tearin' down th' little bit of respectability that a body's thryin' to build up? Am I always goin' to be havin' to nurse yous into th' hardy habit o' thryin' to keep up a little bit of appearance?

The Covey. Why weren't you here to see th' way he run at me with th' sword?

Peter. What did you call me a lemon-whiskered oul' swine for?

Nora. If th' two o' yous don't thry to make a generous, altheration in your goin's on, an' keep on thryin' t' inaugurate th' customs o' th' rest o' th' house into this place, yous can flit into other lodgin's where your bowsey battlin' 'ill meet, maybe, with an encore.

Peter (to Nora). Would you like to be called a lemon-whiskered oul' swine?

Nora. If you attempt to wag that sword of yours at anybody again, it'll have to be taken off you an' put in a safe place away from babies that don't know th' danger o' them things.

Peter. (at entrance to room, Back). Well, I'm not goin' to let anybody call me a lemon-whiskered oul' swine.   [*He goes in.*

Fluther (trying the door). Openin' an' shuttin' now with a well-mannered motion, like a door of a select bar in a high-class pub.

Nora (to the Covey, *as she lays table for tea).* An', once for all, Willie, you'll have to thry to deliver yourself from th' desire of provokin' oul' Pether into a wild forgetfulness of what's proper an' allowable in a respectable home.

The Covey. Well, let him mind his own business, then. Yestherday I caught him hee-hee-in' out of him an' he readin' bits out of Jenersky's *Thesis on th' Origin, Development, an' Consolidation of th' Evolutionary Idea of th' Proletariat.*

Nora. Now, let it end at that, for God's sake; Jack'll be in any minute, an' I'm not goin' to have th' quiet of his evenin' tossed about in an everlastin' uproar between you an' Uncle Pether. (*To* Fluther) Well, did you manage to settle th' lock, yet, Mr. Good?

Fluther (opening and shutting door). It's betther than a new one, now, Mrs. Clitheroe; it's almost ready to open and shut of its own accord.

Nora (giving him a coin). You're a whole man. How many pints will that get you?

Fluther (seriously). Ne'er a one at all, Mrs. Clitheroe, for Fluther's on th' wather waggon now. You could stan' where you're stannin' chantin', 'Have a glass o' malt, Fluther; Fluther, have a glass o' malt,' till th' bells would be ringin' th' ould year out an' th' New Year in, an' you'd have as much chance o' movin' Fluther as a tune on a tin whistle would move a deaf man an' he dead.

[*As* Nora *is opening and shutting door,* Mrs. Bessie Burgess
*appears at it. She is a woman of forty, vigorously built.
Her face is a dogged one, hardened by toil, and a little
coarsened by drink. She looks scornfully and viciously at*
Nora *for a few moments before she speaks.*

Bessie. Puttin' a new lock on her door . . . afraid her
poor neighbours ud break through an' steal. . . . (*In a loud
tone*) Maybe, now, they're a damn sight more honest than your
ladyship . . . checkin' th' children playin' on th' stairs . . .
gettin' on th' nerves of your ladyship. . . . Complainin' about
Bessie Burgess singin' her hymns at night, when she has a few
up. . . . (*She comes in half-way on the threshold, and screams*)
Bessie Burgess 'll sing whenever she damn well likes!

[Nora *tries to shut the door, but* Bessie *violently shoves it in,
and, gripping* Nora *by the shoulders, shakes her.*

Bessie. You little over-dressed throllop, you, for one pin
I'd paste th' white face o' you!

Nora (*frightened*). Fluther, Fluther!

Fluther (*running over and breaking the hold of* Bessie *from* Nora).
Now, now, Bessie, Bessie, leave poor Mrs. Clitheroe alone;
she'd do no one any harm, an' minds no one's business but her
own.

Bessie. Why is she always thryin' to speak proud things,
an' lookin' like a mighty one in th' congregation o' th' people!

[Nora *sinks frightened on to the couch as* Jack Clitheroe
*enters. He is a tall, well-made fellow of twenty-five. His
face has none of the strength of* Nora's. *It is a face in
which is the desire for authority, without the power to attain
it.*

Clitheroe (*excitedly*). What's up? what's afther happenin'?

Fluther. Nothin', Jack. Nothin'. It's all over now.
Come on, Bessie, come on.

Clitheroe (*to* Nora). What's wrong, Nora? Did she say
anything to you?

Nora. She was bargin' out of her, an' I only told her to

g'up ower o' that to her own place; an' before I knew where I was, she flew at me like a tiger, an' thried to guzzle me!

Clitheroe (going to door and speaking to Bessie). Get up to your own place, Mrs. Burgess, and don't you be interferin' with my wife, or it'll be th' worse for you. . . . Go on, go on!

Bessie (as Clitheroe is pushing her out). Mind who you're pushin', now. . . . I attend me place o' worship, anyhow . . . not like some o' them that go to neither church, chapel nor meetin'-house. . . . If me son was home from th' threnches he'd see me righted.

[*Bessie and Fluther depart, and Clitheroe closes the door.*

Clitheroe (going over to Nora, and putting his arm round her). There, don't mind that old bitch, Nora, darling; I'll soon put a stop to her interferin'.

Nora. Some day or another, when I'm here be meself, she'll come in an' do somethin' desperate.

Clitheroe (kissing her). Oh, sorra fear of her doin' anythin' desperate. I'll talk to her to-morrow when she's sober. A taste o' me mind that'll shock her into the sensibility of behavin' herself!

[*Nora gets up and settles the table. She sees the dungarees on the floor and stands looking at them, then she turns to the Covey, who is reading Jenersky's 'Thesis' at the fire.*

Nora. Willie, is that th' place for your dungarees?

The Covey (getting up and lifting them from the floor). Ah, they won't do th' floor any harm, will they?

[*He carries them into room, Back.*

Nora (calling). Uncle Peter, now, Uncle Peter; tea's ready.

[*Peter and the Covey come in from room, Back; they all sit down to tea. Peter is in full dress of the Foresters: green coat, gold braided; white breeches, top boots, frilled shirt. He carries the slouch hat, with the white ostrich plume, and the sword in his hands. They eat for a few moments in silence, the Covey furtively looking at Peter with scorn in his eyes. Peter knows it and is fidgety.*

The Covey (*provokingly*). Another cut o' bread, Uncle Peter?   [*Peter maintains a dignified silence.*

Clitheroe. It's sure to be a great meetin' to-night. We ought to go, Nora.

Nora (*decisively*). I won't go, Jack; you can go if you wish.

The Covey. D'ye want th' sugar, Uncle Peter?   [*A pause.*

Peter (*explosively*). Now, are you goin' to start your thryin' an' your twartin' again?

Nora. Now, Uncle Peter, you mustn't be so touchy; Willie has only assed you if you wanted th' sugar.

Peter. He doesn't care a damn whether I want th' sugar or no. He's only thryin' to twart me!

Nora (*angrily, to the* Covey). Can't you let him alone, Willie? If he wants the sugar, let him stretch his hand out an' get it himself!

The Covey (*to* Peter). Now, if you want the sugar, you can stretch out your hand and get it yourself!

Clitheroe. To-night is th' first chance that Brennan has got of showing himself off since they made a Captain of him— why, God only knows. It'll be a treat to see him swankin' it at th' head of the Citizen Army carryin' th' flag of the Plough an' th' Stars. . . . (*Looking roguishly at* Nora) He was sweet on you, once, Nora?

Nora. He may have been. . . . I never liked him. I always thought he was a bit of a thick.

The Covey. They're bringin' nice disgrace on that banner now.

Clitheroe (*remonstratively*). How are they bringin' disgrace on it?

The Covey (*snappily*). Because it's a Labour flag, an' was never meant for politics. . . . What does th' design of th' field plough, bearin' on it th' stars of th' heavenly plough, mean, if it's not Communism? It's a flag that should only be used when we're buildin' th' barricades to fight for a Workers' Republic!

Peter (with a puff of derision). P-phuh.

The Covey (angrily). What are you phuhin' out o' you for? Your mind is th' mind of a mummy. *(Rising)* I betther go an' get a good place to have a look at Ireland's warriors passin' by.   [*He goes into room, Left, and returns with his cap.*

Nora (to the Covey). Oh, Willie, brush your clothes before you go.

The Covey. Oh, they'll do well enough.

Nora. Go an' brush them; th' brush is in th' drawer there.
        [*The* Covey *goes to the drawer, muttering, gets the brush, and starts to brush his clothes.*

The Covey (singing at Peter, as he does so):

> Oh, where's th' slave so lowly,
> Condemn'd to chains unholy,
> Who, could he burst his bonds at first,
> Would pine beneath them slowly?
>
> We tread th' land that . . . bore us,
> Th' green flag glitters . . . o'er us,
> Th' friends we've tried are by our side,
> An' th' foe we hate . . . before us!

Peter (leaping to his feet in a whirl of rage). Now, I'm tellin' you, me young Covey, once for all, that I'll not stick any longer these tittherin' taunts of yours, rovin' around to sing your slights an' slandhers, reddenin' th' mind of a man to th' thinkin' an' sayin' of things that sicken his soul with sin! *(Hysterical; lifting up a cup to fling at the Covey)* Be God, I'll——

Clitheroe (catching his arm). Now then, none o' that, none o' that!

Nora. Uncle Pether, Uncle Pether, UNCLE PETHER!

The Covey (at the door, about to go out). Isn't that th' malignant oul' varmint! Lookin' like th' illegitimate son of an illegitimate child of a corporal in th' Mexican army!

                [*He goes out.*

Peter (*plaintively*). He's afther leavin' me now in such a state of agitation that I won't be able to do meself justice when I'm marchin' to th' meetin'.

Nora (*jumping up*). Oh, for God's sake, here, buckle your sword on, and go to your meetin', so that we'll have at least one hour of peace!   [*She proceeds to belt on the sword.*

Clitheroe (*irritably*). For God's sake hurry him up ou' o' this, Nora.

Peter. Are yous all goin' to thry to start to twart me now?

Nora (*putting on his plumed hat*). S-s-sh. Now, your hat's on, your house is thatched; off you pop!

[*She gently pushes him from her.*

Peter (*going, and turning as he reaches the door*). Now, if that young Covey——

Nora. Go on, go on.   [*He goes.*

[*Clitheroe sits down in the lounge, lights a cigarette, and looks thoughtfully into the fire. Nora takes the things from the table, placing them on the chest of drawers. There is a pause, then she swiftly comes over to him and sits beside him.*

Nora (*softly*). A penny for them, Jack!

Clitheroe. Me? Oh, I was thinkin' of nothing.

Nora. You were thinkin' of th' . . . meetin' . . . Jack. When we were courtin' an' I wanted you to go, you'd say, 'Oh, to hell with meetin's,' an' that you felt lonely in cheerin' crowds when I was absent. An' we weren't a month married when you began that you couldn't keep away from them.

Clitheroe. Oh, that's enough about th' meetin'. It looks as if you wanted me to go th' way you're talkin'. You were always at me to give up th' Citizen Army, an' I gave it up; surely that ought to satisfy you.

Nora. Ay, you gave it up—because you got th' sulks when they didn't make a Captain of you. It wasn't for my sake, Jack.

Clitheroe. For your sake or no, you're benefitin' by it,

aren't you? I didn't forget this was your birthday, did I?
(*He puts his arms around her*) And you liked your new hat;
didn't you, didn't you? [*He kisses her rapidly several times.*

Nora (*panting*). Jack, Jack; please, Jack! I thought you
were tired of that sort of thing long ago.

Clitheroe. Well, you're finding out now that I amn't tired of
it yet, anyhow. Mrs. Clitheroe doesn't want to be kissed, sure
she doesn't? (*He kisses her again*) Little, little red-lipped Nora!

Nora (*coquettishly removing his arm from around her*). Oh, yes,
your little, little red-lipped Nora's a sweet little girl when th'
fit seizes you; but your little, little red-lipped Nora has to clean
your boots every mornin', all the same.

Clitheroe (*with a movement of irritation*). Oh, well, if we're
goin' to be snotty! [*A pause.*

Nora. It's lookin' like as if it was you that was goin' to
be . . . snotty! Bridlin' up with bittherness, th' minute a
body attempts t' open her mouth.

Clitheroe. Is it any wondher, turnin' a tendher sayin' into
a meanin' o' malice an' spite!

Nora. It's hard for a body to be always keepin' her mind
bent on makin' thoughts that'll be no longer than th' length
of your own satisfaction. [*A pause.*

Nora (*standing up*). If we're goin' to dhribble th' time away
sittin' here like a pair o' cranky mummies, I'd be as well
sewin' or doin' something about th' place.

[*She looks appealingly at him for a few moments; he doesn't
speak. She swiftly sits down beside him, and puts her arm
around his neck.*

Nora (*imploringly*). Ah, Jack, don't be so cross!

Clitheroe (*doggedly*). Cross? I'm not cross; I'm not a bit
cross. It was yourself started it.

Nora (*coaxingly*). I didn't mean to say anything out o'
the way. You take a body up too quickly, Jack. (*In an
ordinary tone as if nothing of an angry nature had been said*) You
didn't offer me me evenin' allowance yet.

[*Clitheroe silently takes out a cigarette for her and himself and lights both.*

Nora (*trying to make conversation*).   How quiet th' house is now; they must be all out.

Clitheroe (*rather shortly*).   I suppose so.

Nora (*rising from the seat*).   I'm longin' to show you me new hat, to see what you think of it.   Would you like to see it?

Clitheroe.   Ah, I don't mind.

[*Nora suppresses a sharp reply, hesitates for a moment, then gets the hat, puts it on, and stands before* Clitheroe.

Nora.   Well, how does Mr. Clitheroe like me new hat?

Clitheroe.   It suits you, Nora, it does right enough.

[*He stands up, puts his hand beneath her chin, and tilts her head up. She looks at him roguishly.   He bends down and kisses her.*

Nora.   Here, sit down, an' don't let me hear another cross word out of you for th' rest o' the night.   [*They sit down.*

Clitheroe (*with his arms around her*).   Little, little, red-lipped Nora!

Nora (*with a coaxing movement of her body towards him*).   Jack!

Clitheroe (*tightening his arms around her*).   Well?

Nora.   You haven't sung me a song since our honeymoon. Sing me one now, do . . . please, Jack!

Clitheroe.   What song?   'Since Maggie Went Away'?

Nora.   Ah, no, Jack, not that; it's too sad.   'When You said You Loved Me.'

[*Clearing his throat,* Clitheroe *thinks for a moment and then begins to sing.   Nora, putting an arm around him, nestles her head on his breast and listens delightedly.*

Clitheroe (*singing verses following to the air of 'When You and I were Young, Maggie*):

    Th' violets were scenting th' woods, Nora,
        Displaying their charm to th' bee,
    When I first said I lov'd only you, Nora,
        An' you said you lov'd only me!

Th' chestnut blooms gleam'd through th' glade,
        Nora,
    A robin sang loud from a tree,
When I first said I lov'd only you, Nora,
    An' you said you lov'd only me!

Th' golden-rob'd daffodils shone, Nora,
    An' danc'd in th' breeze on th' lea,
When I first said I lov'd only you, Nora,
    An' you said you lov'd only me!

Th' trees, birds, an' bees sang a song, Nora,
    Of happier transports to be,
When I first said I lov'd only you, Nora,
    An' you said you lov'd only me!

[*Nora kisses him.*
[*A knock is heard at the door, Right; a pause as they listen.*
    Nora clings closely to Clitheroe. *Another knock, more*
    imperative than the first.

Clitheroe. I wonder who can that be, now?

Nora (a little nervous). Take no notice of it, Jack; they'll
go away in a minute.   [*Another knock, followed by a voice.*

Voice. Commandant Clitheroe, Commandant Clitheroe,
are you there? A message from General Jim Connolly.

Clitheroe. Damn it, it's Captain Brennan.

Nora (anxiously). Don't mind him, don't mind, Jack.
Don't break our happiness. . . . Pretend we're not in. Let
us forget everything to-night but our two selves!

Clitheroe (reassuringly). Don't be alarmed, darling; I'll
just see what he wants, an' send him about his business.

Nora (tremulously). No, no. Please, Jack; don't open it.
Please, for your own little Nora's sake!

Clitheroe (rising to open the door). Now don't be silly, Nora.
    [Clitheroe *opens the door, and admits a young man in the full*
        uniform of the Irish Citizen Army—green suit; slouch

green hat caught up at one side by a small Red Hand badge; Sam Browne belt, with a revolver in the holster. He carries a letter in his hand. When he comes in he smartly salutes Clitheroe. The young man is Captain Brennan.

Capt. Brennan (giving the letter to Clitheroe). A dispatch from General Connolly.

Clitheroe (reading. While he is doing so, Brennan's *eyes are fixed on* Nora, *who droops as she sits on the lounge).* 'Commandant Clitheroe is to take command of the eighth battalion of the I.C.A. which will assemble to proceed to the meeting at nine o'clock. He is to see that all units are provided with full equipment; two days' rations and fifty rounds of ammunition. At two o'clock A.M. the army will leave Liberty Hall for a reconnaissance attack on Dublin Castle.—Com.-Gen. Connolly.'

Clitheroe. I don't understand this. Why does General Connolly call me Commandant?

Capt. Brennan. Th' Staff appointed you Commandant, and th' General agreed with their selection.

Clitheroe. When did this happen?

Capt. Brennan. A fortnight ago.

Clitheroe. How is it word was never sent to me?

Capt. Brennan. Word was sent to you. . . . I meself brought it.

Clitheroe. Who did you give it to, then?

Capt. Brennan (after a pause). I think I gave it to Mrs. Clitheroe, there.

Clitheroe. Nora, d'ye hear that?   [Nora *makes no answer.*

Clitheroe (there is a note of hardness in his voice). Nora . . . Captain Brennan says he brought a letter to me from General Connolly, and that he gave it to you. . . . Where is it? What did you do with it?

Nora (running over to him, and pleadingly putting her arms around him). Jack, please, Jack, don't go out to-night an'

I'll tell you; I'll explain everything. . . . Send him away, an' stay with your own little red-lipp'd Nora.

Clitheroe (*removing her arms from around him*). None o' this nonsense, now; I want to know what you did with th' letter?

[*Nora goes slowly to the lounge and sits down.*

Clitheroe (*angrily*). Why didn't you give me th' letter? What did you do with it? . . . (*He shakes her by the shoulder*) What did you do with th' letter?

Nora (*flaming up*). I burned it, I burned it! That's what I did with it! Is General Connolly an' th' Citizen Army goin' to be your only care? Is your home goin' to be only a place to rest in? Am I goin' to be only somethin' to provide merry-makin' at night for you? Your vanity'll be th' ruin of you an' me yet. . . . That's what's movin' you: because they've made an officer of you, you'll make a glorious cause of what you're doin', while your little red-lipp'd Nora can go on sittin' here, makin' a companion of th' loneliness of th' night!

Clitheroe (*fiercely*). You burned it, did you? (*He grips her arm*) Well, me good lady——

Nora. Let go—you're hurtin' me!

Clitheroe. You deserve to be hurt. . . . Any letter that comes to me for th' future, take care that I get it. . . . D'ye hear—take care that I get it!

[*He goes to the chest of drawers and takes out a Sam Browne belt, which he puts on, and then puts a revolver in the holster. He puts on his hat, and looks towards Nora. While this dialogue is proceeding, and while Clitheroe prepares himself, Brennan softly whistles 'The Soldiers' Song'.*

Clitheroe (*at door, about to go out*). You needn't wait up for me; if I'm in at all, it won't be before six in th' morning.

Nora (*bitterly*). I don't care if you never come back!

Clitheroe (*to* Capt. Brennan). Come along, Ned.

[*They go out; there is a pause. Nora pulls her new hat from her head and with a bitter movement flings it to the*

*other end of the room. There is a gentle knock at door,
Right, which opens, and Mollser comes into the room.
She is about fifteen, but looks to be only about ten, for the
ravages of consumption have shrivelled her up. She is
pitifully worn, walks feebly, and frequently coughs. She
goes over to Nora.*

Mollser (*to* Nora). Mother's gone to th' meetin', an' I
was feelin' terrible lonely, so I come down to see if you'd let
me sit with you, thinkin' you mightn't be goin' yourself. . . .
I do be terrible afraid I'll die sometime when I'm be meself.
. . . I often envy you, Mrs. Clitheroe, seein' th' health you
have, an' th' lovely place you have here, an' wondherin' if I'll
ever be sthrong enough to be keepin' a home together for a
man. Oh, this must be some more o' the Dublin Fusiliers
flyin' off to the front.

> [*Just before* Mollser *ceases to speak, there is heard in the
> distance the music of a brass band playing a regiment to
> the boat on the way to the front. The tune that is being
> played is 'It's a Long Way to Tipperary'; as the band
> comes to the chorus, the regiment is swinging into the street
> by* Nora's *house, and the voices of the soldiers can be heard
> lustily singing the chorus of the song.*

It's a long way to Tipperary, it's a long way to go;
It's a long way to Tipperary, to th' sweetest girl I know!
Goodbye, Piccadilly; farewell, Leicester Square.
It's a long, long way to Tipperary, but my heart's right
    there!

> [Nora *and* Mollser *remain silently listening. As the chorus
> ends and the music is faint in the distance again,* Bessie
> Burgess *appears at door, Right, which* Mollser *has left
> open.*

Bessie (*speaking in towards the room*). There's th' men
marchin' out into th' dhread dimness o' danger, while th'
lice is crawlin' about feedin' on th' fatness o' the land! But

yous'll not escape from th' arrow that flieth be night, or th' sickness that wasteth be day. . . . An' ladyship an' all, as some o' them may be, they'll be scattered abroad, like th' dust in th' darkness!

> [Bessie *goes away;* Nora *steals over and quietly shuts the door. She comes back to the lounge and wearily throws herself on it beside* Mollser.

Mollser (*after a pause and a cough*). Is there anybody goin', Mrs. Clitheroe, with a titther o' sense?

CURTAIN

ACT II

A commodious public-house at the corner of the street in which the meeting is being addressed from Platform No. 1. It is the south corner of the public-house that is visible to the audience. The counter, beginning at Back about one-fourth of the width of the space shown, comes across two-thirds of the length of the stage, and, taking a circular sweep, passes out of sight to Left. On the counter are beer-pulls, glasses, and a carafe. The other three-fourths of the Back is occupied by a tall, wide, two-paned window. Beside this window at the Right is a small, box-like, panelled snug. Next to the snug is a double swing door, the entrance to that particular end of the house. Farther on is a shelf on which customers may rest their drinks. Underneath the windows is a cushioned seat. Behind the counter at Back can be seen the shelves running the whole length of the counter. On these shelves can be seen the end (or the beginning) of rows of bottles. The Barman *is seen wiping the part of the counter which is in view.* Rosie *is standing at the counter toying with what remains of a half of whisky in a wine-glass. She is a sturdy, well-shaped girl of twenty; pretty, and pert in manner. She is wearing a cream blouse, with an obviously suggestive glad neck; a grey tweed dress, brown stockings and shoes. The blouse and most of the dress are hidden by a black shawl. She has no hat, and in her hair is jauntily set a cheap, glittering, jewelled ornament. It is an hour later.*

Barman (*wiping counter*). Nothin' much doin' in your line to-night, Rosie?

Rosie. Curse o' God on th' haporth, hardly, Tom. There isn't much notice taken of a pretty petticoat of a night like this. . . . They're all in a holy mood. Th' solemn-lookin' dials on th' whole o' them an' they marchin' to th' meetin'. You'd think they were th' glorious company of th' saints, an' th' noble army of martyrs thrampin' through th' sthreets of paradise. They're all thinkin' of higher things than a girl's garthers. . . . It's a tremendous meetin'; four platforms they have—there's one o' them just outside opposite th' window.

Barman. Oh, ay; sure when th' speaker comes (*motioning with his hand*) to th' near end, here, you can see him plain, an' hear nearly everythin' he's spoutin' out of him.

Rosie. It's no joke thryin' to make up fifty-five shillin's a week for your keep an' laundhry, an' then taxin' you a quid for your own room if you bring home a friend for th' night. . . . If I could only put by a couple of quid for a swankier outfit, everythin' in th' garden ud look lovely——

Barman. Whisht, till we hear what he's sayin'.

[*Through the window is silhouetted the figure of a tall man who is speaking to the crowd. The* Barman *and* Rosie *look out of the window and listen.*

The Voice of the Man. It is a glorious thing to see arms in the hands of Irishmen. We must accustom ourselves to the thought of arms, we must accustom ourselves to the sight of arms, we must accustom ourselves to the use of arms. . . . Bloodshed is a cleansing and sanctifying thing, and the nation that regards it as the final horror has lost its manhood. . . . There are many things more horrible than bloodshed, and slavery is one of them!

[*The figure moves away towards the Right, and is lost to sight and hearing.*

Rosie. It's th' sacred thruth, mind you, what that man's afther sayin'.

Barman. If I was only a little younger, I'd be plungin' mad into th' middle of it!

Rosie (*who is still looking out of the window*). Oh, here's the two gems runnin' over again for their oil!

[Peter *and* Fluther *enter tumultuously. They are hot, and full and hasty with the things they have seen and heard. Emotion is bubbling up in them, so that when they drink,*

and when they speak, they drink and speak with the
fullness of emotional passion. Peter leads the way to the
counter.

Peter (*splutteringly to* Barman). Two halves . . . (*To*
Fluther) A meetin' like this always makes me feel as if I could
dhrink Loch Erinn dhry!

Fluther. You couldn't feel any way else at a time like this
when th' spirit of a man is pulsin' to be out fightin' for th'
thruth with his feet thremblin' on th' way, maybe to th'
gallows, an' his ears tinglin' with th' faint, far-away sound of
burstin' rifle-shots that'll maybe whip th' last little shock o' life
out of him that's left lingerin' in his body!

Peter. I felt a burnin' lump in me throat when I heard
th' band playin' 'The Soldiers' Song', rememberin' last
hearin' it marchin' in military formation with th' people
starin' on both sides at us, carryin' with us th' pride an' resolu-
tion o' Dublin to th' grave of Wolfe Tone.

Fluther. Get th' Dublin men goin' an' they'll go on full
force for anything that's thryin' to bar them away from
what they're wantin', where th' slim thinkin' counthry boyo
ud limp away from th' first faintest touch of compromization!

Peter (*hurriedly to the* Barman). Two more, Tom! . . .
(*To* Fluther) Th' memory of all th' things that was done, an'
all th' things that was suffered be th' people, was boomin' in
me brain. . . . Every nerve in me body was quiverin' to do
somethin' desperate!

Fluther. Jammed as I was in th' crowd, I listened to th'
speeches pattherin' on th' people's head, like rain fallin' on
th' corn; every derogatory thought went out o' me mind, an'
I said to meself, 'You can die now, Fluther, for you've seen th'
shadow-dhreams of th' past leppin' to life in th' bodies of livin'
men that show, if we were without a titther o' courage for
centuries, we're vice versa now!' Looka here. (*He stretches
out his arm under* Peter's *face and rolls up his sleeve.*) The blood
was BOILIN' in me veins!

[*The silhouette of the tall figure again moves into the frame of the window speaking to the people.*

Peter (*unaware, in his enthusiasm, of the speaker's appearance, to* Fluther). I was burnin' to dhraw me sword, an' wave an' wave it over me——

Fluther (*overwhelming* Peter). Will you stop your blatherin' for a minute, man, an' let us hear what he's sayin'!

Voice of the Man. Comrade soldiers of the Irish Volunteers and of the Citizen Army, we rejoice in this terrible war. The old heart of the earth needed to be warmed with the red wine of the battlefields. . . . Such august homage was never offered to God as this: the homage of millions of lives given gladly for love of country. And we must be ready to pour out the same red wine in the same glorious sacrifice, for without shedding of blood there is no redemption!

[*The figure moves out of sight and hearing.*

Fluther (*gulping down the drink that remains in his glass, and rushing out*). Come on, man; this is too good to be missed!

[Peter *finishes his drink less rapidly, and as he is going out wiping his mouth with the back of his hand he runs into the* Covey *coming in. He immediately erects his body like a young cock, and with his chin thrust forward, and a look of venomous dignity on his face, he marches out.*

The Covey (*at counter*). Give us a glass o' malt, for God's sake, till I stimulate meself from the shock o' seein' th' sight that's afther goin' out!

Rosie (*all business, coming over to the counter, and standing near the* Covey). Another one for me, Tommy; (*to the* Barman) th' young gentleman's ordherin' it in th' corner of his eye.

[*The* Barman *brings the drink for the* Covey, *and leaves it on the counter.* Rosie *whips it up.*

Barman. Ay, houl' on there, houl' on there, Rosie!

Rosie (*to the* Barman). What are you houldin' on out o' you for? Didn't you hear th' young gentleman say that he couldn't refuse anything to a nice little bird? (*To the* Covey)

Isn't that right, Jiggs? (*The* Covey *says nothing.*) Didn't I know, Tommy, it would be all right? It takes Rosie to size a young man up, an' tell th' thoughts that are thremblin' in his mind. Isn't that right, Jiggs?

[*The* Covey *stirs uneasily, moves a little farther away, and pulls his cap over his eyes.*

Rosie (*moving after him*). Great meetin' that's gettin' held outside. Well, it's up to us all, anyway, to fight for our freedom.

The Covey (*to* Barman). Two more, please. (*To Rosie*) Freedom! What's th' use o' freedom, if it's not economic freedom?

Rosie (*emphasizing with extended arm and moving finger*). I used them very words just before you come in. 'A lot o' thricksters,' says I, 'that wouldn't know what freedom was if they got it from their mother.' . . . (*To* Barman) Didn't I, Tommy?

Barman. I disremember.

Rosie. No, you don't disremember. Remember you said, yourself, it was all 'only a flash in th' pan'. Well, 'flash in th' pan, or no flash in th' pan,' says I, 'they're not goin' to get Rosie Redmond,' says I, 'to fight for freedom that wouldn't be worth winnin' in a raffle!'

The Covey. There's only one freedom for th' workin' man: conthrol o' th' means o' production, rates of exchange, an' th' means of disthribution. (*Tapping* Rosie *on the shoulder*) Look here, comrade, I'll leave here to-morrow night for you a copy of Jenersky's *Thesis on the Origin, Development, an' Consolidation of the Evolutionary Idea of the Proletariat.*

Rosie (*throwing off her shawl on to the counter, and showing an exemplified glad neck, which reveals a good deal of a white bosom*). If y'ass Rosie, it's heartbreakin' to see a young fella thinkin' of anything, or admirin' anything, but silk thransparent stockin's showin' off the shape of a little lassie's legs!

[*The* Covey, *frightened, moves a little away.*

Rosie (following on). Out in th' park in th' shade of a warm summery evenin', with your little darlin' bridie to be, kissin' an' cuddlin' (*she tries to put her arm around his neck*), kissin' an' cuddlin', ay?

The Covey (frightened). Ay, what are you doin'? None o' that, now; none o' that. I've something else to do besides shinannickin' afther Judies!

[*He turns away, but Rosie follows, keeping face to face with him.*

Rosie. Oh, little duckey, oh, shy little duckey! Never held a mot's hand, an' wouldn't know how to tittle a little Judy! (*She clips him under the chin.*) Tittle him undher th' chin, tittle him undher th' chin!

The Covey (breaking away and running out). Ay, go on, now; I don't want to have any meddlin' with a lassie like you!

Rosie (enraged). Jasus, it's in a monasthery some of us ought to be, spendin' our holidays kneelin' on our adorers, tellin' our beads, an' knockin' hell out of our buzzums!

The Covey (outside). Cuckoo-oo!

[*Peter and Fluther come in again, followed by Mrs. Gogan, carrying a baby in her arms. They go over to the counter.*

Peter (with plaintive anger). It's terrible that young Covey can't let me pass without proddin' at me! Did you hear him murmurin' 'cuckoo' when we were passin'?

Fluther (irritably). I wouldn't be everlastin' cockin' me ear to hear every little whisper that was floatin' around about me! It's my rule never to lose me temper till it would be dethrimental to keep it. There's nothin' derogatory in th' use o' th' word 'cuckoo', is there?

Peter (tearfully). It's not th' word; it's th' way he says it: he never says it straight out, but murmurs it with curious quiverin' ripples, like variations on a flute!

Fluther. Ah, what odds if he gave it with variations on a thrombone! (*To Mrs. Gogan*) What's yours goin' to be, ma'am?

Mrs. Gogan. Ah, a half o' malt, Fluther.

Fluther (to Barman) Three halves, Tommy.

[*The* Barman *brings the drinks.*

Mrs. Gogan (drinking). The Foresthers' is a gorgeous dhress! I don't think I've seen nicer, mind you, in a pantomime. . . . Th' loveliest part of th' dhress, I think, is th' osthrichess plume. . . . When yous are goin' along, an' I see them wavin' an' noddin' an' waggin', I seem to be lookin' at each of yous hangin' at th' end of a rope, your eyes bulgin' an' your legs twistin' an' jerkin', gaspin' an' gaspin' for. breath while yous are thryin' to die for Ireland!

Fluther. If any o' them is hangin' at the end of a rope, it won't be for Ireland!

Peter. Are you goin' to start th' young Covey's game o' proddin' an' twartin' a man? There's not many that's talkin' can say that for twenty-five years he never missed a pilgrimage to Bodenstown!

Fluther. You're always blowin' about goin' to Bodenstown. D'ye think no one but yourself ever went to Bodenstown?

Peter (plaintively). I'm not blowin' about it; but there's not a year that I go there but I pluck a leaf off Tone's grave, an' this very day me prayer-book is nearly full of them.

Fluther (scornfully). Then Fluther has a vice versa opinion of them that put ivy leaves into their prayer-books, scabbin' it on th' clergy, an' thryin' to out-do th' haloes o' th' saints be lookin' as if he was wearin' around his head a glittherin' aroree boree allis! *(Fiercely)* Sure, I don't care a damn if you slep' in Bodenstown! You can take your breakfast, dinner, an' tea on th' grave in Bodenstown, if you like, for Fluther!

Mrs. Gogan. Oh, don't start a fight, boys, for God's sake; I was only sayin' what a nice costume it is—nicer than th' kilts, for, God forgive me, I always think th' kilts is hardly decent.

Fluther. Ah, sure, when you'd look at him, you'd wondher

whether th' man was makin' fun o' th' costume, or th' costume was makin' fun o' th' man!

Barman. Now, then, thry to speak asy, will yous? We don't want no shoutin' here.

> [*The* Covey *followed by* Bessie Burgess *comes in. They go over to the opposite end of the counter, and direct their gaze on the other group.*

The Covey (*to* Barman). Two glasses o' malt.

Peter. There he is, now; I knew he wouldn't be long till he folleyed me in.

Bessie (*speaking to the* Covey, *but really at the other party*). I can't for th' life o' me undherstand how they can call themselves Catholics, when they won't lift a finger to help poor little Catholic Belgium.

Mrs. Gogan. (*raising her voice*). What about poor little Catholic Ireland?

Bessie (*over to* Mrs. Gogan). You mind your own business, ma'am, an' stupefy your foolishness be gettin' dhrunk.

Peter (*anxiously*). Take no notice of her; pay no attention to her. She's just tormentin' herself towards havin' a row with somebody.

Bessie. There's a storm of anger tossin' in me heart, thinkin' of all th' poor Tommies, an' with them me own son, dhrenched in water an' soaked in blood, gropin' their way to a shattherin' death, in a shower o' shells! Young men with th' sunny lust o' life beamin' in them, layin' down their white bodies, shredded into torn an' bloody pieces, on th' althar that God Himself has built for th' sacrifice of heroes!

Mrs. Gogan. Isn't it a nice thing to have to be listenin' to a lassie an' hangin' our heads in a dead silence, knowin' that some persons think more of a ball of malt than they do of th' blessed saints.

Fluther. Whisht; she's always dangerous an' derogatory when she's well oiled. Th' safest way to hindher her from havin' any enjoyment out of her spite, is to dip our thoughts

into the fact of her bein' a female person that has moved out
of th' sight of ordinary sensible people.

Bessie. To look at some o' th' women that's knockin'
about, now, is a thing to make a body sigh. . . . A woman
on her own, dhrinkin' with a bevy o' men, is hardly an example
to her sex. . . . A woman dhrinkin' with a woman is one
thing, an' a woman dhrinkin' with herself is still a woman—
flappers may be put in another category altogether—but a
middle-aged married woman makin' herself th' centre of a
circle of men is as a woman that is loud an' stubborn, whose
feet abideth not in her own house.

The Covey (*to* Bessie). When I think of all th' problems in
front o' th' workers, it makes me sick to be lookin' at oul'
codgers goin' about dhressed up like green-accoutred figures
gone asthray out of a toyshop!

Peter. Gracious God, give me patience to be listenin' to
that blasted young Covey proddin' at me from over at th'
other end of th' shop!

Mrs. Gogan (*dipping her finger in the whisky, and moistening
with it the lips of her baby*). Cissie Gogan's a woman livin' for
nigh on twenty-five years in her own room, an' beyond biddin'
th' time o' day to her neighbours, never yet as much as nodded
her head in th' direction of other people's business, while she
knows some as are never content unless they're standin'
senthry over other people's doin's!

> [Bessie *is about to reply, when the tall, dark figure is again
> silhouetted against the window, and the voice of the
> speaker is heard speaking passionately.*

Voice of Speaker. The last sixteen months have been the
most glorious in the history of Europe. Heroism has come
back to the earth. War is a terrible thing, but war is not an
evil thing. People in Ireland dread war because they do not
know it. Ireland has not known the exhilaration of war for
over a hundred years. When war comes to Ireland she must
welcome it as she would welcome the Angel of God!

[*The figure passes out of sight and hearing.*

The Covey (*towards all present*). Dope, dope. There's only one war worth havin': th' war for th' economic emancipation of th' proletariat.

Bessie. They may crow away out o' them; but it ud be fitther for some o' them to mend their ways, an' cease from havin' scouts out watchin' for th' comin' of th' Saint Vincent de Paul man, for fear they'd be nailed lowerin' a pint of beer, mockin' th' man with an angel face, shinin' with th' glamour of deceit an' lies!

Mrs. Gogan. An' a certain lassie standin' stiff behind her own door with her ears cocked listenin' to what's being said, stuffed till she's sthrained with envy of a neighbour thryin' for a few little things that may be got be hard sthrivin' to keep up to th' letther an' th' law, an' th' practices of th' Church!

Peter (*to* Mrs. Gogan). If I was you, Mrs. Gogan, I'd parry her jabbin' remarks be a powerful silence that'll keep her tantalizin' words from penethratin' into your feelin's. It's always betther to leave these people to th' vengeance o' God!

Bessie. Bessie Burgess doesn't put up to know much, never havin' a swaggerin' mind, thanks be to God, but goin' on packin' up knowledge accordin' to her conscience: precept upon precept, line upon line; here a little, an there a little. But (*with a passionate swing of her shawl*), thanks be to Christ, she knows when she was got, where she was got, an' how she was got; while there's some she knows, decoratin' their finger with a well-polished weddin' ring, would be hard put to it if they were assed to show their weddin' lines!

Mrs. Gogan (*plunging out into the centre of the floor in a wild tempest of hysterical rage*). Y' oul' rip of a blasted liar, me weddin' ring's been well earned be twenty years be th' side o' me husband, now takin' his rest in heaven, married to me be Father Dempsey, in th' Chapel o' Saint Jude's, in th' Christmas Week of eighteen hundhred an' ninety-five; an' any kid, livin' or dead, that Jinnie Gogan's had since, was got

between th' bordhers of th' Ten Commandments! . . . An'
that's more than some o' you can say that are kep' from th'
dhread o' desthruction be a few drowsy virtues, that th' first
whisper of temptation lulls into a sleep, that'll know one sin
from another only on th' day of their last anointin', an' that
use th' innocent light o' th' shinin' stars to dip into th' sins of
a night's diversion!

Bessie (*jumping out to face* Mrs. Gogan, *and bringing the palms
of her hands together in sharp claps to emphasize her remarks*).   Liar
to you, too, ma'am, y' oul' hardened thresspasser on other
people's good nature, wizenin' up your soul in th' arts o'
dodgeries, till every dhrop of respectability in a female is
dhried up in her, lookin' at your ready-made manœuverin'
with th' menkind!

Barman.   Here, there; here, there; speak asy there.   No
rowin' here, no rowin' here, now.

Fluther (*trying to calm* Mrs. Gogan).   Now Jinnie, Jinnie,
it's a derogatory thing to be smirchin' a night like this with a
row; it's rompin' with th' feelin's of hope we ought to be,
instead o' bein' vice versa!

Peter (*trying to quiet* Bessie).   I'm terrible dawny, Mrs.
Burgess, an' a fight leaves me weak for a long time afther-
wards. . . . Please, Mrs. Burgess, before there's damage done,
try to have a little respect for yourself.

Bessie (*with a push of her hand that sends* Peter *tottering to the
end of the shop*).   G'way, you little sermonizing, little yella-
faced, little consequential, little pudgy, little bum, you!

Mrs. Gogan (*screaming*).   Fluther, leggo!   I'm not goin' to
keep an unresistin' silence, an' her scattherin' her festherin'
words in me face, stirrin' up ever dhrop of decency in a respectable female, with her restless rally o' lies that would make
a saint say his prayer backwards!

Bessie (*shouting*).   Ah, everybody knows well that th' best
charity that can be shown to you is to hide th' thruth as much
as our thrue worship of God Almighty will allow us!

Mrs. Gogan (frantically). Here, houl' th' kid, one o' yous; houl' th' kid for a minute! There's nothin' for it but to show this lassie a lesson or two. . . . (*To* Peter) Here, houl' th' kid, you. (*Before* Peter *is aware of it, she places the infant in his arms.*)

Mrs. Gogan (to Bessie, *standing before her in a fighting attitude*). Come on, now, me loyal lassie, dyin' with grief for little Catholic Belgium! When Jinnie Gogan's done with you, you'll have a little leisure lyin' down to think an' pray for your king an' counthry!

Barman (coming from behind the counter, getting between the women, and proceeding to push them towards the door). Here, now, since yous can't have a little friendly argument quietly, you'll get out o' this place in quick time. Go on, an' settle your differences somewhere else—I don't want to have another endorsement on me licence.

Peter (anxiously, over to Mrs. Gogan). Here, take your kid back, ower this. How nicely I was picked, now, for it to be plumped into me arms!

The Covey. She knew who she was givin' it to, maybe.

Peter (hotly to the Covey). Now, I'm givin' you fair warnin', me young Covey, to quit firin' your jibes an' jeers at me. . . . For one o' these days, I'll run out in front o' God Almighty an' take your sacred life!

Barman (pushing Bessie *out after* Mrs. Gogan). Go on, now; out you go.

Bessie (as she goes out). If you think, me lassie, that Bessie Burgess has an untidy conscience, she'll soon show you to th' differ!

Peter (leaving the baby down on the floor). Ay, be Jasus, wait there, till I give her back her youngster! (*He runs to the door.*) Ay, there, ay! (*He comes back.*) There, she's afther goin' without her kid. What are we goin' to do with it, now?

The Covey. What are we goin' to do with it? Bring it outside an' show everybody what you're afther findin'!

Peter (*in a panic to* Fluther).   Pick it up, you, Fluther, an'
run afther her with it, will you?

Fluther.   What d'ye take Fluther for?   You must think
Fluther's a right gom.   D'ye think Fluther's like yourself,
destitute of a titther of undherstandin'?

Barman (*imperatively to* Peter).   Take it up, man, an' run out
afther her with it, before she's gone too far.   You're not goin'
to leave th' bloody thing here, are you?

Peter (*plaintively, as he lifts up the baby*).   Well, God Almighty,
give me patience with all th' scorners, tormentors, an' twarters
that are always an' ever thryin' to goad me into prayin' for
their blindin' an' blastin' an' burnin' in th' world to come!

                                                    [*He goes out.*

Fluther.   God, it's a relief to get rid o' that crowd.   Women
is terrible when they start to fight.   There's no holdin'
them back.   (*To the* Covey) Are you goin' to have anything?

The Covey.   Ah, I don't mind if I have another half.

Fluther (*to* Barman).   Two more, Tommy, me son.

                                          [*The* Barman *gets the drinks.*

Fluther.   You know, there's no conthrollin' a woman when
she loses her head.

        [Rosie *enters and goes over to the counter on the side nearest*
            to Fluther.

Rosie (*to* Barman).   Divil a use i' havin' a thrim little leg
on a night like this; things was never worse. . . . Give us a
half till to-morrow, Tom, duckey.

Barman (*coldly*).   No more to-night, Rosie; you owe me for
three already.

Rosie (*combatively*).   You'll be paid, won't you?

Barman.   I hope so.

Rosie.   You hope so!   Is that th' way with you, now?

Fluther (*to* Barman).   Give her one; it'll be all right.

Rosie (*clapping* Fluther *on the back*).   Oul' sport!

Fluther.   Th' meetin' should be soon over, now.

The Covey. Th' sooner th' betther. It's all a lot o' blasted nonsense, comrade.

Fluther. Oh, I wouldn't say it was all nonsense. Afther all, Fluther can remember th' time, an' him only a dawny chiselur, bein' taught at his mother's knee to be faithful to th' Shan Van Vok!

The Covey. That's all dope, comrade; th' sort o' thing that workers are fed on be th' Boorzwawzee.

Fluther (a little sharply). What's all dope? Though I'm sayin' it that shouldn't: (*catching his cheek with his hand, and pulling down the flesh from the eye*) d'ye see that mark there, undher me eye? . . . A sabre slice from a dragoon in O'Connell Street! (*Thrusting his head forward towards* Rosie) Feel that dint in th' middle o' me nut!

Rosie (rubbing Fluther's *head, and winking at the* Covey). My God, there's a holla!

Fluther (putting on his hat with quiet pride). A skelp from a bobby's baton at a Labour meetin' in th' Phœnix Park!

The Covey. He must ha' hitten you in mistake. I don't know what you ever done for th' Labour movement.

Fluther (loudly). D'ye not? Maybe, then, I done as much, an' know as much about th' Labour movement as th' chancers that are blowin' about it!

Barman. Speak easy, Fluther, thry to speak easy.

The Covey. There's no necessity to get excited about it, comrade.

Fluther (more loudly). Excited? Who's gettin' excited? There's no one gettin' excited! It would take something more than a thing like you to flutther a feather o' Fluther. Blatherin', an', when all is said, you know as much as th' rest in th' wind up!

The Covey. Well, let us put it to th' test, then, an' see what you know about th' Labour movement: what's the mechanism of exchange?

Fluther (roaring, because he feels he is beaten). How th' hell do I know what it is?   There's nothin' about that in th' rules of our Thrades Union!

Barman.   For God's sake, thry to speak easy, Fluther.

The Covey.   What does Karl Marx say about th' Relation of Value to th' Cost o' Production?

Fluther (*angrily*).   What th' hell do I care what he says? I'm Irishman enough not to lose me head be follyin' foreigners!

Barman.   Speak easy, Fluther.

The Covey.   It's only waste o' time talkin' to you, comrade.

Fluther.   Don't be comradin' me, mate.   I'd be on me last legs if I wanted you for a comrade.

Rosie (*to the* Covey).   It seems a highly rediculous thing to hear a thing that's only an inch or two away from a kid, swingin' heavy words about he doesn't know th' meanin' of, an' uppishly thryin' to down a man like Misther Fluther here, that's well flavoured in th' knowledge of th' world he's livin in.

The Covey (*savagely to* Rosie).   Nobody's askin' you to be buttin' in with your prate. . . . I have you well taped, me lassie. . . . Just you keep your opinions for your own place. . . . It'll be a long time before th' Covey takes any insthructions or reprimandin' from a prostitute!

Rosie (*wild with humiliation*).   You louse, you louse, you! . . . You're no man. . . . You're no man . . . I'm a woman, anyhow, an' if I'm a prostitute aself, I have me feelin's. . . . Thryin' to put his arm around me a minute ago, an' givin' me th' glad eye, th' little wrigglin' lump o' desolation turns on me now, because he saw there was nothin' doin'. . . . You louse, you!   If I was a man, or you were a woman, I'd bate th' puss o' you!

Barman.   Ay, Rosie, ay!   You'll have to shut your mouth altogether, if you can't learn to speak easy!

Fluther (*to* Rosie).   Houl' on there, Rosie; houl' on there. There's no necessity to flutther yourself when you're with Fluther. . . . Any lady that's in th' company of Fluther is goin' to get a fair hunt. . . . This is outside your province.

. . . I'm not goin' to let you demean yourself be talkin' to a tittherin' chancer. . . . Leave this to Fluther—this is a man's job. (*To the* Covey) Now, if you've anything to say, say it to Fluther, an', let me tell you, you're not goin' to be pass-remarkable to any lady in my company.

The Covey. Sure I don't care if you were runnin' all night afther your Mary o' th' Curlin' Hair, but, when you start tellin' luscious lies about what you done for th' Labour move-ment, it's nearly time to show y'up!

Fluther (*fiercely*). Is it you show Fluther up? G'way, man, I'd beat two o' you before me breakfast!

The Covey (*contemptuously*). Tell us where you bury your dead, will you?

Fluther (*with his face stuck into the face of the* Covey). Sing a little less on th' high note, or, when I'm done with you, you'll put a Christianable consthruction on things, I'm tellin' you!

The Covey. You're a big fella, you are.

Fluther (*tapping the* Covey *threateningly on the shoulder*). Now, you're temptin' Providence when you're temptin' Fluther!

The Covey (*losing his temper, and bawling*). Easy with them hands, there, easy with them hands! You're startin' to take a little risk when you commence to paw the Covey!

[Fluther *suddenly springs into the middle of the shop, flings his hat into the corner, whips off his coat, and begins to paw the air.*

Fluther (*roaring at the top of his voice*). Come on, come on, you lowser; put your mits up now, if there's a man's blood in you! Be God, in a few minutes you'll see some snots flyin' around, I'm tellin' you. . . . When Fluther's done with you, you'll have a vice versa opinion of him! Come on, now, come on!

Barman (*running from behind the counter and catching hold of the* Covey). Here, out you go, me little bowsey. Because you got a couple o' halves you think you can act as you like. (*He pushes the* Covey *to the door*) Fluther's a friend o' mine, an' I'll not have him insulted.

The Covey (struggling with the Barman). Ay, leggo, leggo there; fair hunt, give a man a fair hunt! One minute with him is all I ask; one minute alone with him, while you're runnin' for th' priest an' th' doctor.

Fluther (to the Barman). Let him go, let him go, Tom! let him open th' door to sudden death if he wants to!

Barman (to the Covey). Go on, out you go an' do th' bowsey somewhere else. [*He pushes the* Covey *out and comes back.*

Rosie (getting Fluther's *hat as he is putting on his coat*). Be God, you put th' fear o' God in his heart that time! I thought you'd have to be dug out of him. . . . Th' way you lepped out without any of your fancy side-steppin'! 'Men like Fluther,' say I to meself, 'is gettin' scarce nowadays.'

Fluther (with proud complacency). I wasn't goin' to let meself be malignified by a chancer. . . . He got a little bit too derogatory for Fluther. . . . Be God, to think of a cur like that comin' to talk to a man like me!

Rosie (fixing on his hat). Did j'ever!

Fluther. He's lucky he got off safe. I hit a man last week, Rosie, an' he's fallin' yet!

Rosie. Sure, you'd ha' broken him in two if you'd ha' hitten him one clatther!

Fluther (amorously, putting his arm around Rosie). Come on into th' snug, me little darlin', an' we'll have a few dhrinks before I see you home.

Rosie. Oh, Fluther, I'm afraid you're a terrible man for th' women.

> [*The go into the snug as* Clitheroe, Captain Brennan, *and* Lieut. Langon *of the Irish Volunteers enter hurriedly.* Captain Brennan *carries the banner of The Plough and the Stars, and* Lieut. Langon *a green, white, and orange Tri-colour. They are in a state of emotional excitement. Their faces are flushed and their eyes sparkle; they speak rapidly, as if unaware of the meaning of what they said. They have been mesmerized by the fervency of the speeches.*

Clitheroe (almost pantingly).   Three glasses o' port!

[*The* Barman *brings the drinks.*

Capt. Brennan.   We won't have long to wait now.

Lieut. Langon.   Th' time is rotten ripe for revolution.

Clitheroe.   You have a mother, Langon.

Lieut. Langon.   Ireland is greater than a mother.

Capt. Brennan.   You have a wife, Clitheroe.

Clitheroe.   Ireland is greater than a wife.

Lieut. Langon.   Th' time for Ireland's battle is now—th' place for Ireland's battle is here.

[*The tall, dark figure again is silhouetted against the window. The three men pause and listen.*

Voice of the Man.   Our foes are strong, but strong as they are, they cannot undo the miracles of God, who ripens in the heart of young men the seeds sown by the young men of a former generation.   They think they have pacified Ireland; think they have foreseen everything; think they have provided against everything; but the fools, the fools, the fools!— they have left us our Fenian dead, and, while Ireland holds these graves, Ireland, unfree, shall never be at peace!

Capt. Brennan (*catching up The Plough and the Stars*).   Imprisonment for th' Independence of Ireland!

Lieut. Langon (catching up the Tri-colour).   Wounds for th' Independence of Ireland!

Clitheroe.   Death for th' Independence of Ireland!

The Three (together).   So help us God!

[*They drink.   A bugle blows the Assembly.   They hurry out.   A pause.   Fluther and Rosie come out of the snug; Rosie is linking Fluther, who is a little drunk.   Both are in a merry mood.*

Rosie.   Come on home, ower o' that, man.   Are you afraid or what?   Are you goin' to come home, or are you not?

Fluther.   Of course I'm goin' home.   What ud ail me that I wouldn't go?

Rosie (lovingly).   Come on, then, oul' sport.

Officer's Voice (giving command outside). Irish Volunteers, by th' right, quick march!

Rosie (putting her arm round Fluther *and singing):*

I once had a lover, a tailor, but he could do nothin' for me,
An' then I fell in with a sailor as strong an' as wild as th'
    sea.
We cuddled an' kissed with devotion, till th' night from
    th' mornin' had fled;
An' there, to our joy, a bright bouncin' boy
Was dancin' a jig in th' bed!

Dancin' a jig in th' bed, an' bawlin' for butther an' bread.
An' there, to our joy, a bright bouncin' boy
Was dancin' a jig in th' bed!

[*They go out with their arms round each other.*
Clitheroe's Voice (in command outside). Dublin Battalion of the Irish Citizen Army, by th' right, quick march!

CURTAIN

ACT III

The corner house in a street of tenements: it is the home of the Clitheroes. The house is a long, gaunt, five-story tenement; its brick front is chipped and scarred with age and neglect. The wide and heavy hall door, flanked by two pillars, has a look of having been charred by a fire in the distant past. The door lurches a little to one side, disjointed by the continual and reckless banging when it is being closed by most of the residents. The diamond-paned fanlight is destitute of a single pane, the framework alone remaining. The windows, except the two looking into the front parlour (Clitheroe's room), are grimy, and are draped with fluttering and soiled fragments of lace curtains. The front parlour windows are hung with rich, comparatively, casement cloth. Five stone steps lead from the door to the path on the street. Branching on each side are railings to prevent people from falling into the area. At the left corner of the house runs a narrow lane, bisecting the street, and connecting it with another of the same kind. At the corner of the lane is a street lamp.

As the house is revealed, Mrs. Gogan *is seen helping* Mollser *to a chair, which stands on the path beside the railings, at the left side of the steps. She then wraps a shawl around* Mollser's *shoulders. It is some months later.*

Mrs. Gogan (arranging shawl around Mollser). Th' sun'll do you all th' good in th' world. A few more weeks o' this weather, an' there's no knowin' how well you'll be. . . . Are you comfy, now?

Mollser (weakly and wearily). Yis, ma; I'm all right.

Mrs. Gogan. How are you feelin'?

Mollser. Betther, ma, betther. If th' horrible sinkin' feelin' ud go, I'd be all right.

Mrs. Gogan. Ah, I wouldn't put much pass on that. Your

stomach maybe's out of ordher. . . . Is th' poor breathin'
any betther, d'ye think?

Mollser. Yis, yis, ma; a lot betther.

Mrs. Gogan. Well, that's somethin' anyhow. . . . With
th' help o' God, you'll be on th' mend from this out. . . .
D'your legs feel any sthronger undher you, d'ye think!

Mollser (*irritably*). I can't tell, ma. I think so. . . . A
little.

Mrs. Gogan. Well, a little aself is somethin'. . . . I thought
I heard you coughin' a little more than usual last night. . . .
D'ye think you were?

Mollser. I wasn't, ma, I wasn't.

Mrs. Gogan. I thought I heard you, for I was kep' awake
all night with th' shootin'. An' thinkin' o' that madman,
Fluther, runnin' about through th' night lookin' for Nora
Clitheroe to bring her back when he heard she'd gone to folly
her husband, an' in dhread any minute he might come
staggerin' in covered with bandages, splashed all over with th'
red of his own blood, an' givin' us barely time to bring th'
priest to hear th' last whisper of his final confession, as his soul
was passin' through th' dark doorway o' death into th' way
o' th' wondherin' dead. . . . You don't feel cold, do you?

Mollser. No, ma; I'm all right.

Mrs. Gogan. Keep your chest well covered, for that's th'
delicate spot in you . . . if there's any danger, I'll whip you
in again. . . . (*Looking up the street*) Oh, here's th' Covey an'
oul' Pether hurryin' along. God Almighty, sthrange things
is happenin' when them two is pullin' together.

[*The* Covey *and* Peter *come in, breathless and excited.*

Mrs. Gogan (*to the two men*). Were yous far up th' town?
Did yous see any sign o' Fluther or Nora? How is things
lookin'? I hear they're blazin' away out o' th' G.P.O.
That th' Tommies is sthretched in heaps around Nelson's
Pillar an' th' Parnell Statue, an' that th' pavin' sets in
O'Connell Street is nearly covered be pools o' blood.

Peter. We seen no sign o' Nora or Fluther anywhere.

Mrs. Gogan. We should ha' held her back be main force from goin' to look for her husband. . . . God knows what's happened to her—I'm always seein' her sthretched on her back in some hospital, moanin' with th' pain of a bullet in her vitals, an' nuns thryin' to get her to take a last look at th' crucifix!

The Covey. We can do nothin'. You can't stick your nose into O'Connell Street, an' Tyler's is on fire.

Peter. An' we seen th' Lancers——

The Covey (interrupting). Throttin' along, heads in th' air; spurs an' sabres jinglin', an' lances quiverin', an' lookin' as if they were assin' themselves, 'Where's these blighters, till we get a prod at them?' when there was a volley from th' Post Office that stretched half o' them, an' sent th' rest gallopin' away wondherin' how far they'd have to go before they'd feel safe.

Peter (rubbing his hands). 'Damn it,' says I to meself, 'this looks like business!'

The Covey. An' then out comes General Pearse an' his staff, an', standin' in th' middle o' th' street, he reads th' Proclamation.

Mrs. Gogan. What proclamation?

Peter. Declarin' an Irish Republic.

Mrs. Gogan. Go to God!

Peter. The gunboat *Helga's* shellin' Liberty Hall, an' I hear the people livin' on th' quays had to crawl on their bellies to Mass with th' bullets that were flyin' around from Boland's Mills.

Mrs. Gogan. God bless us, what's goin' to be th' end of it all!

Bessie (looking out of the top window). Maybe yous are satisfied now; maybe yous are satisfied now. Go on an' get guns if yous are men—Johnny get your gun, get your gun, get your gun! Yous are all nicely shanghaied now; th' boyo hasn't a sword on his thigh now! Oh, yous are all nicely shanghaied now!

Mrs. Gogan (warningly to Peter *and the* Covey). S-s-sh, don't answer her. She's th' right oul' Orange bitch! She's been chantin' 'Rule, Britannia' all th' mornin'.

Peter. I hope Fluther hasn't met with any accident, he's such a wild card.

Mrs. Gogan. God grant it; but last night I dreamt I seen gettin' carried into th' house a sthretcher with a figure lyin' on it, stiff an' still, dhressed in th' habit of Saint Francis. An' then, I heard th' murmurs of a crowd no one could see sayin' th' litany for th' dead; an' then it got so dark that nothin' was seen but th' white face of th' corpse, gleamin' like a white wather-lily floatin' on th' top of a dark lake. Then a tiny whisper thrickled into me ear, sayin', 'Isn't the face very like th' face o' Fluther?' an' then, with a thremblin' flutther, th' dead lips opened, an' although I couldn't hear, I knew they were sayin', 'Poor oul' Fluther, afther havin' handed in his gun at last, his shakin' soul moored in th' place where th' wicked are at rest an' th' weary cease from throublin'.'

Peter (who has put on a pair of spectacles, and has been looking down the street). Here they are, be God, here they are; just afther turnin' th' corner—Nora an' Fluther!

The Covey. She must be wounded or something—he seems to be carryin' her.

> [Fluther *and* Nora *enter.* Fluther *has his arm around her and is half leading, half carrying her in. Her eyes are dim and hollow, her face pale and strained-looking; her hair is tossed, and her clothes are dusty.*

Mrs. Gogan (running over to them). God bless us, is it wounded y'are, Mrs. Clitheroe, or what?

Fluther. Ah, she's all right, Mrs. Gogan; only worn out from thravellin' an' want o' sleep. A night's rest, now, an' she'll be as fit as a fiddle. Bring her in, an' make her lie down.

Mrs. Gogan (*to* Nora). Did you hear e'er a whisper o' Mr. Clitheroe?

Nora (*wearily*). I could find him nowhere, Mrs. Gogan. None o' them would tell me where he was. They told me I shamed my husband an' th' women of Ireland be carryin' on as I was. . . . They said th' women must learn to be brave an' cease to be cowardly. . . . Me who risked more for love than they would risk for hate. . . . (*Raising her voice in hysterical protest*) My Jack will be killed, my Jack will be killed! . . . He is to be butchered as a sacrifice to th' dead!

Bessie (*from upper window*). Yous are all nicely shanghaied now! Sorra mend th' lasses that have been kissin' an' cuddlin' their boys into th' sheddin' of blood! . . . Fillin' their minds with fairy tales that had no beginnin', but, please God, 'll have a bloody quick endin'! . . . Turnin' bitther into sweet, an' sweet into bitther. . . . Stabbin' in th' back th' men that are dyin' in th' threnches for them! It's a bad thing for any one that thries to jilt th' Ten Commandments, for judgements are prepared for scorners an' sthripes for th' back o' fools! (*Going away from window as she sings*):

> Rule, Britannia, Britannia rules th' waves,
> Britons never, never, never shall be slaves!

Fluther (*with a roar up at the window*). Y'ignorant oul' throllop, you!

Mrs. Gogan (*to* Nora). He'll come home safe enough to you, you'll find, Mrs. Clitheroe; afther all, there's a power o' women that's handed over sons an' husbands to take a runnin' risk in th' fight they're wagin'.

Nora. I can't help thinkin' every shot fired 'll be fired at Jack, an' every shot fired at Jack 'll be fired at me. What do I care for th' others? I can think only of me own self. . . . An' there's no woman gives a son or a husband to be killed— if they say it, they're lyin', lyin', against God, Nature, an' against themselves! . . . One blasted hussy at a barricade

told me to go home an' not be thryin' to dishearten th' men.
. . . That I wasn't worthy to bear a son to a man that was
out fightin' for freedom. . . . I clawed at her, an' smashed
her in th' face till we were separated. . . . I was pushed
down th' street, an' I cursed them—cursed the rebel ruffians
an' Volunteers that had dhragged me ravin' mad into th'
sthreets to seek me husband!

Peter. You'll have to have patience, Nora. We all have
to put up with twarthers an' tormentors in this world.

The Covey. If they were fightin' for anything worth while,
I wouldn't mind.

Fluther (*to* Nora). Nothin' derogatory 'll happen to Mr.
Clitheroe. You'll find, now, in th' finish up it'll be vice versa.

Nora. Oh, I know that wherever he is, he's thinkin' of
wantin' to be with me. I know he's longin' to be passin' his
hand through me hair, to be caressin' me neck, to fondle me
hand an' to feel me kisses clingin' to his mouth. . . . An' he
stands wherever he is because he's brave? (*Vehemently*) No,
but because he's a coward, a coward, a coward!

Mrs. Gogan. Oh, they're not cowards anyway.

Nora (*with denunciatory anger*). I tell you they're afraid to
say they're afraid! . . . Oh, I saw it, I saw it, Mrs. Gogan.
. . . At th' barricade in North King Street I saw fear glowin'
in all their eyes. . . . An' in th' middle o' th' sthreet was
somethin' huddled up in a horrible tangled heap. . . . His
face was jammed again th' stones, an' his arm was twisted
round his back. . . . An' every twist of his body was a cry
against th' terrible thing that had happened to him. . . . An'
I saw they were afraid to look at it. . . . An' some o' them
laughed at me, but th' laugh was a frightened one. . . . An'
some o' them shouted at me, but th' shout had in it th' shiver
o' fear. . . . I tell you they were afraid, afraid, afraid!

Mrs. Gogan (*leading her towards the house*). Come on in,
dear. If you'd been a little longer together, th' wrench
asundher wouldn't have been so sharp.

Nora. Th' agony I'm in since he left me has thrust away every rough thing he done, an' every unkind word he spoke; only th' blossoms that grew out of our lives are before me now; shakin' their colours before me face, an' breathin' their sweet scent on every thought springin' up in me mind, till, sometimes, Mrs. Gogan, sometimes I think I'm goin' mad!

Mrs. Gogan. You'll be a lot betther when you have a little lie down.

Nora (turning towards Fluther *as she is going in).* I don't know what I'd have done, only for Fluther. I'd have been lyin' in th' streets, only for him. . . . *(As she goes in)* They have dhriven away th' little happiness life had to spare for me. He has gone from me for ever, for ever. . . . Oh, Jack, Jack, Jack!

[*She is led in by* Mrs. Gogan, *as* Bessie *comes out with a shawl around her shoulders. She passes by them with her head in the air. When they have gone in, she gives a mug of milk to* Mollser *silently.*

Fluther. Which of yous has th' tossers?

The Covey. I have.

Bessie (as she is passing them to go down the street). You an' your Leadhers an' their sham-battle soldiers has landed a body in a nice way, havin' to go an' ferret out a bit o' bread God knows where. . . . Why aren't yous in th' G.P.O. if yous are men? It's paler an' paler yous are gettin'. . . . A lot o' vipers, that's what th' Irish people is!   [*She goes out.*

Fluther. Never mind her. . . . *(To the* Covey*)* Make a start an' keep us from th' sin o' idleness. *(To* Mollser*)* Well, how are you to-day, Mollser, oul' son? What are you dhrinkin', milk?

Mollser. Grand, Fluther, grand, thanks. Yis, milk.

Fluther. You couldn't get a betther thing down you. . . . This turn-up has done one good thing, anyhow; you can't get dhrink anywhere, an' if it lasts a week, I'll be so used to it that I won't think of a pint.

The Covey (*who has taken from his pocket two worn coins and a thin strip of wood about four inches long*).   What's th' bettin'?

Peter.   Heads, a juice.

Fluther.   Harps, a tanner.

> [*The* Covey *places the coins on the strip of wood, and flips them up into the air.   As they jingle on the ground the distant boom of a big gun is heard.   They stand for a moment listening.*

Fluther.   What th' hell's that?

The Covey.   It's like th' boom of a big gun!

Fluther.   Surely to God they're not goin' to use artillery on us?

The Covey (*scornfully*).   Not goin'!   (*Vehemently*) Wouldn't they use anything on us, man?

Fluther.   Aw, holy Christ, that's not playin' th' game!

Peter (*plaintively*).   What would happen if a shell landed here now?

The Covey (*ironically*).   You'd be off to heaven in a fiery chariot.

Peter.   In spite of all th' warnin's that's ringin' around us, are you goin' to start your pickin' at me again?

Fluther.   Go on, toss them again, toss them again. . . . Harps, a tanner.

Peter.   Heads, a juice.   [*The* Covey *tosses the coins.*

Fluther (*as the coins fall*).   Let them roll, let them roll.   Heads, be God!

> [Bessie *runs in excitedly.   She has a new hat on her head, a fox fur round her neck over her shawl, three umbrellas under her right arm, and a box of biscuits under her left.   She speaks rapidly and breathlessly.*

Bessie.   They're breakin' into th' shops, they're breakin' into th' shops!   Smashin' th' windows, battherin' in th' doors, an' whippin' away everything!   An' th' Volunteers is firin' on them.   I seen two men an' a lassie pushin' a piano down th' sthreet, an' th' sweat rollin' off them thryin' to get it up on th' pavement; an' an oul' wan that must ha' been seventy lookin' as if she'd dhrop every minute with th' dint o' heart beatin', thryin' to pull a big double bed out of a broken shop-window! I was goin' to wait till I dhressed meself from th' skin out.

Mollser (*to Bessie, as she is going in*).   Help me in, Bessie; I'm feelin' curious.

[*Bessie leaves the looted things in the house, and, rapidly returning, helps* Mollser *in.*

The Covey.   Th' selfishness of that one—she waited till she got all she could carry before she'd come to tell anyone!

Fluther (*running over to the door of the house and shouting in to* Bessie).   Ay, Bessie, did you hear of e'er a pub gettin' a shake up?

Bessie (*inside*).   I didn't hear o' none.

Fluther (*in a burst of enthusiasm*).   Well, you're goin' to hear of one soon!

The Covey.   Come on, man, an' don't be wastin' time.

Peter (*to them as they are about to run off*).   Ay, ay, are you goin' to leave me here?

Fluther.   Are you goin' to leave yourself here?

Peter (*anxiously*).   Didn't yous hear her sayin' they were firin' on them?

The Covey and Fluther (*together*).   Well?

Peter.   Supposin' I happened to be potted?

Fluther.   We'd give you a Christian burial, anyhow.

The Covey (*ironically*).   Dhressed up in your regimentals.

Peter (*to the* Covey, *passionately*).   May th' all-lovin' God give you a hot knock one o' these days, me young Covey, tuthorin' Fluther up now to be tiltin' at me, an' crossin' me with his mockeries an' jibin'!

[*A fashionably dressed, middle-aged, stout woman comes hurriedly in, and makes for the group. She is almost fainting with fear.*

The Woman.   For Gawd's sake, will one of you kind men

show any safe way for me to get to Wrathmines? . . . I was foolish enough to visit a friend, thinking the howl thing was a joke, and now I cawn't get a car or a tram to take me home— isn't it awful?

Fluther. I'm afraid, ma'am, one way is as safe as another.

Woman. And what am I gowing to do? Oh, isn't this awful? . . . I'm so different from others. . . . The mowment I hear a shot, my legs give way under me—I cawn't stir, I'm paralysed—isn't it awful?

Fluther (*moving away*). It's a derogatory way to be, right enough, ma'am.

Woman (*catching Fluther's coat*). Creeping along the street there, with my head down and my eyes half shut, a bullet whizzed past within an inch of my nowse. . . . I had to lean against the wall for a long time, gasping for breath—I nearly passed away—it was awful! . . . I wonder, would you kind men come some of the way and see me safe?

Fluther. I have to go away, ma'am, to thry an' save a few things from th' burnin' buildin's.

The Covey. Come on, then, or there won't be anything left to save.   [*The* Covey *and* Fluther *hurry away.*

Woman (*to* Peter). Wasn't it an awful thing for me to leave my friend's house? Wasn't it an idiotic thing to do? . . . I haven't the slightest idea where I am. . . . You have a kind face, sir. Could you possibly come and pilot me in the direction of Wrathmines?

Peter (*indignantly*). D'ye think I'm goin' to risk me life throttin' in front of you? An' maybe get a bullet that would gimme a game leg or something that would leave me a jibe an' a jeer to Fluther an' th' young Covey for th' rest o' me days!

    [*With an indignant toss of his head he walks into the house.*

The Woman (*going out*). I know I'll fall down in a dead faint if I hear another shot go off anyway near me—isn't it awful!

    [Mrs. Gogan *comes out of the house pushing a pram before her. As she enters the street,* Bessie *rushes out, follows*

Mrs. Gogan, *and catches hold of the pram, stopping* Mrs. Gogan's *progress.*

Bessie. Here, where are you goin' with that? How quick you were, me lady, to clap your eyes on th' pram. . . . Maybe you don't know that Mrs. Sullivan, before she went to spend Easther with her people in Dunboyne, gave me sthrict injunctions to give an accasional look to see if it was still standin' where it was left in th' corner of th' lobby.

Mrs. Gogan. That remark of yours, Mrs. Bessie Burgess, requires a little considheration, seein' that th' pram was left on our lobby, an' not on yours; a foot or two a little to th' left of th' jamb of me own room door; nor is it needful to mention th' name of th' person that gave a squint to see if it was there th' first thing in th' mornin', an' th' last thing in th' stillness o' th' night; never failin' to realize that her eyes couldn't be goin' wrong, be sthretchin' out her arm an' runnin' her hand over th' pram, to make sure that th' sight was no deception! Moreover, somethin's tellin' me that th' runnin' hurry of an inthrest you're takin' in it now is a sudden ambition to use th' pram for a purpose that a loyal woman of law an' ordher would stagger away from!

[*She gives the pram a sudden push that pulls* Bessie *forward.*

Bessie (*still holding the pram*). There's not as much as one body in th' house that doesn't know that it wasn't Bessie Burgess that was always shakin' her voice complainin' about people leavin' bassinettes in th' way of them that, week in an' week out, had to pay their rent, an' always had to find a regular accommodation for her own furniture in her own room. . . . An' as for law an' ordher, puttin' aside th' harp an' shamrock, Bessie Burgess 'll have as much respect as she wants for th' lion an' unicorn!

Peter (*appearing at the door*). I think I'll go with th' pair of yous an' see th' fun. A fella might as well chance it, anyhow.

Mrs. Gogan (*taking no notice of* Peter, *and pushing the pram on another step*). Take your rovin' lumps o' hands from pattin' th' bassinette, if you please, ma'am; an', steppin' from th' threshold of good manners, let me tell you, Mrs. Burgess, that it's a fat wondher to Jennie Gogan that a lady-like singer o' hymns like yourself would lower her thoughts from sky-thinkin' to stretch out her arm in a sly-seekin' way to pinch anything dhriven asthray in th' confusion of th' battle our boys is makin' for th' freedom of their counthry!

Peter (*laughing and rubbing his hands together*).   Hee, hee, hee, hee, hee!   I'll go with th' pair o' yous an' give yous a hand.

Mrs. Gogan (*with a rapid turn of her head as she shoves the pram forward*).   Get up in th' prambulator an' we'll wheel you down.

Bessie (*to Mrs. Gogan*).   Poverty an' hardship has sent Bessie Burgess to abide with sthrange company, but she always knew them she had to live with from backside to break-fast time; an' she can tell them, always havin' had a Christian kinch on her conscience, that a passion for thievin' an' pinchin' would find her soul a foreign place to live in, an' that her present intention is quite th' lofty-hearted one of pickin' up anything shaken up an' scatthered about in th' loose confusion of a general plundher!

> [*By this time they have disappeared from view. Peter is following, when the boom of a big gun in the distance brings him to a quick halt.*

Peter.   God Almighty, that's th' big gun again!   God forbid any harm would happen to them, but sorra mind I'd mind if they met with a dhrop in their mad endeyvours to plundher an' desthroy.

> [*He looks down the street for a moment, then runs to the hall door of the house, which is open, and shuts it with a vicious pull; he then goes to the chair in which* Mollser *had sat, sits down, takes out his pipe, lights it and begins to smoke with his head carried at a haughty angle. The* Covey *comes staggering in with a ten-stone sack of flour on his back. On the top of the sack is a ham. He goes over to the door,*

*pushes it with his head, and finds he can't open it; he turns
slightly in the direction of* Peter.

The Covey (to Peter). Who shut th' door? . . . (*He kicks
at it*) Here, come on an' open it, will you? This isn't a mot's
hand-bag I've got on me back.

Peter. Now, me young Covey, d'ye think I'm goin' to be
your lackey?

The Covey (angrily). Will you open th' door, y'oul'——

Peter (shouting). Don't be assin' me to open any door,
don't be assin' me to open any door for you. . . . Makin' a
shame an' a sin o' th' cause that good men are fightin' for.
. . . Oh, God forgive th' people that, instead o' burnishin'
th' work th' boys is doin' to-day with quiet honesty an'
patience, is revilin' their sacrifices with a riot of lootin' an'
roguery!

The Covey. Isn't your own eyes leppin' out o' your head
with envy that you haven't th' guts to ketch a few o' th' things
that God is givin' to His chosen people? . . . Y'oul' hypo-
crite, if everyone was blind you'd steal a cross off an ass's back!

Peter (very calmly). You're not going to make me lose me
temper; you can go on with your proddin' as long as you
like; goad an' goad an' goad away; hee, hee, heee! I'll not
lose me temper. [*Somebody opens door and the* Covey *goes in.*

The Covey (inside, mockingly). Cuckoo-oo!

*Peter (running to the door and shouting in a blaze of passion
as he follows the* Covey *in*). You lean, long, lanky lath of a
lowsey bastard. . . . (*Following him in*) Lowsey bastard,
lowsey bastard!

> [Bessie *and* Mrs. Gogan *enter, the pride of a great joy
> illuminating their faces. Bessie is pushing the pram,
> which is filled with clothes and boots; on the top of the
> boots and clothes is a fancy table, which* Mrs. Gogan *is
> holding on with her left hand, while with her right hand
> she holds a chair on the top of her head. They are heard
> talking to each other before they enter.*

...vin' you in th' same danger as themselves. . . . Oh, Jack,
...an't let you go!

Clitheroe.   You must, Nora, you must.

Nora.   All last night at th' barricades I sought you, Jack.
. . I didn't think of th' danger—I could only think of you.
. . I asked for you everywhere. . . . Some o' them
...ughed. . . . I was pushed away, but I shoved back. . . .
...ome o' them even sthruck me . . . an' I screamed an'
...creamed your name!

Clitheroe (in fear her action would give him future shame).
What possessed you to make a show of yourself, like that?
. . . What way d'ye think I'll feel when I'm told my wife
...was bawlin' for me at th' barricades? What are you more
...than any other woman?

Nora.   No more, maybe; but you are more to me than any
other man, Jack. . . . I didn't mean any harm, honestly,
Jack. . . . I couldn't help it. . . . I shouldn't have told you.
. . . My love for you made me mad with terror.

Clitheroe (angrily).   They'll say now that I sent you out th'
way I'd have an excuse to bring you home. . . . Are you
goin' to turn all th' risks I'm takin' into a laugh?

Lieut. Langon.   Let me lie down, let me lie down, Bill;
th' pain would be easier, maybe, lyin' down. . . . Oh, God,
have mercy on me!

Capt. Brennan (to Langon).   A few steps more, Jim, a few
steps more; thry to stick it for a few steps more.

Lieut. Langon.   Oh, I can't, I can't, I can't!

Capt. Brennan (to Clitheroe).   Are you comin', man, or are
you goin' to make an arrangement for another honeymoon?
. . . If you want to act th' renegade, say so, an' we'll be off!

Bessie (from above).   Runnin' from th' Tommies—choke th'
chicken. Runnin' from th' Tommies—choke th' chicken!

Clitheroe (savagely to Brennan).   Damn you, man, who
...vants to act th' renegade? (*To Nora*) Here, let go your hold
...go, I say!

Mrs. Gogan (outside).   I don't remember ever havin' seen
such lovely pairs as them, (*they appear*) with th' pointed toes
an' th' cuban heels.

Bessie.   They'll go grand with th' dhresses we're afther
liftin', when we've stitched a sthray bit o' silk to lift th' bodices
up a little higher, so as to shake th' shame out o' them, an'
make them fit for women that hasn't lost themselves in th'
nakedness o' th' times.

[*They fussily carry in the chair, the table, and some of the
other goods. They return to bring in the rest.*

Peter (at door, sourly to Mrs. Gogan).   Ay, you. Mollser
looks as if she was goin' to faint, an' your youngster is roarin'
in convulsions in her lap.

Mrs. Gogan (snappily).   She's never any other way but
faintin'!

[*She goes to go in with some things in her arms, when a shot
from a rifle rings out. She and Bessie make a bolt for the
door, which Peter, in a panic, tries to shut before they have
got inside.*

Mrs. Gogan.   Ay, ay, ay, you cowardly oul' fool, what are
you thryin' to shut th' door on us for?

[*They retreat tumultuously inside. A pause; then* Captain
Brennan *comes in supporting* Lieutenant Langon,
whose arm is around Brennan's *neck.* Langon's *face,
which is ghastly white, is momentarily convulsed with
spasms of agony. He is in a state of collapse, and*
Brennan *is almost carrying him. After a few moments*
Clitheroe, *pale, and in a state of calm nervousness, follows,
looking back in the direction from which he came, a rifle,
held at the ready, in his hands.*

Capt. Brennan (savagely to Clitheroe).   Why did you fire
over their heads? Why didn't you fire to kill?

Clitheroe.   No, no, Bill; bad as they are they're Irish men
an' women.

Capt. Brennan (savagely).   Irish be damned! Attackin' an' mobbin' th' men that are riskin' their lives for them. If these slum lice gather at our heels again, plug one o' them, or I'll soon shock them with a shot or two meself!

Lieut. Langon (*moaningly*). My God, is there ne'er an ambulance knockin' around anywhere? . . . Th' stomach is ripped out o' me; I feel it—o-o-oh, Christ!

Capt. Brennan. Keep th' heart up, Jim; we'll soon get help, now.

[Nora *rushes wildly out of the house and flings her arms round the neck of* Clitheroe *with a fierce and joyous insistence. Her hair is down, her face is haggard, but her eyes are agleam with the light of happy relief.*

Nora. Jack, Jack, Jack; God be thanked . . . be thanked. . . . He has been kind and merciful to His poor handmaiden. . . . My Jack, my own Jack, that I thought was lost is found, that I thought was dead is alive again! . . . Oh, God be praised for ever, evermore! . . . My poor Jack. . . . Kiss me, kiss me, Jack, kiss your own Nora!

Clitheroe (*kissing her, and speaking brokenly*). My Nora; my little, beautiful Nora, I wish to God I'd never left you.

Nora. It doesn't matter—not now, not now, Jack. It will make us dearer than ever to each other. . . . Kiss me, kiss me again.

Clitheroe. Now, for God's sake, Nora, don't make a scene.

Nora. I won't, I won't; I promise, I promise, Jack; honest to God. I'll be silent an' brave to bear th' joy of feelin' you safe in my arms again. . . . It's hard to force away th' tears of happiness at th' end of an awful agony.

Bessie (*from the upper window*). Th' Minsthrel Boys aren't feelin' very comfortable now. Th' big guns has knocked all th' harps out of their hands. General Clitheroe'd rather be unlacin' his wife's bodice than standin' at a barricade . . . An' th' professor of chicken-butcherin' there, finds he's up against somethin' a little tougher even than his own chickens, an' that's sayin' a lot!

Capt. Brennan (*up to* Bessie). Shut up, y'oul' ha

Bessie (*down to* Brennan). Choke th' chicken, chicken, choke th' chicken!

Lieut. Langon. For God's sake, Bill, bring me where me wound 'll be looked afther. . . . Am before anything is done to save me?

Capt. Brennan (*to* Clitheroe). Come on, Jack. to get help for Jim, here—have you no thought for his danger?

Bessie. Choke th' chicken, choke th' chicken, c chicken!

Clitheroe (*to* Nora). Loosen me, darling, let me go.

Nora (*clinging to him*). No, no, no, I'll not let y Come on, come up to our home, Jack, my sweethea lover, my husband, an' we'll forget th' last few terrible . . . I look tired now, but a few hours of happy rest i arms will bring back th' bloom of freshness again, an' yo be glad, you will be glad, glad . . . glad!

Lieut. Langon. Oh, if I'd kep' down only a little longer, I mightn't ha' been hit! Everyone else escapin', an' me gettin' me belly ripped asundher! . . . I couldn't scream, couldn't even scream. . . . D'ye think I'm really badly wounded, Bill? Me clothes seem to be all soakin' wet. . It's blood . . . My God, it must be me own blood!

Capt. Brennan (*to* Clitheroe). Go on, Jack, bid her g bye with another kiss, an' be done with it! D'ye Langon to die in me arms while you're dallyin' with Nora?

Clitheroe (*to* Nora). I must go, I must go, Nora. I'm we met at all. . . . It couldn't be helped—all other were blocked be th' British. . . . Let me go, can't you, D'ye want me to be unthrue to me comrades?

Nora. No, I won't let you go. . . . I want yo thrue to me, Jack. . . . I'm your dearest comrad your thruest comrade. . . . They only want th' co

Nora (clinging to Clitheroe, and indicating Brennan). Look, Jack, look at th' anger in his face; look at th' fear glintin' in his eyes. . . . He himself's afraid, afraid, afraid! . . . He wants you to go th' way he'll have th' chance of death sthrikin' you an' missin' him! . . . Turn round an' look at him, Jack, look at him, look at him! . . . His very soul is cold . . . shiverin' with th' thought of what may happen to him. . . . It is his fear that is thryin' to frighten you from recognizin' th' same fear that is in your own heart!

Clitheroe (struggling to release himself from Nora). Damn you, woman, will you let me go!

Capt. Brennan (fiercely, to Clitheroe). Why are you beggin' her to let you go? Are you afraid of her, or what? Break her hold on you, man, or go up, an' sit on her lap!

[*Clitheroe trying roughly to break her hold.*

Nora (imploringly). Oh, Jack. . . . Jack. . . . Jack!

Lieut. Langon (agonizingly). Brennan, a priest; I'm dyin', I think, I'm dyin'!

Clitheroe (to Nora). If you won't do it quietly, I'll have to make you! (*To Brennan*) Here, hold this gun, you, for a minute.   [*He hands the gun to Brennan.*

Nora (pitifully). Please, Jack. . . . You're hurting me, Jack. . . . Honestly. . . . Oh, you're hurting . . . me! . . . I won't, I won't, I won't! . . . Oh, Jack, I gave you everything you asked of me. . . . Don't fling me from you, now!

[*He roughly loosens her grip, and pushes her away from him. Nora sinks to the ground and lies there.*

Nora (weakly). Ah, Jack. . . . Jack. . . . Jack!

Clitheroe (taking the gun back from Brennan). Come on, come on.

[*They go out. Bessie looks at Nora lying on the street, for a few moments, then, leaving the window, she comes out, runs over to Nora, lifts her up in her arms, and carries her swiftly into the house. A short pause, then down the*

*street is heard a wild, drunken yell; it comes nearer, and
Fluther enters, frenzied, wild-eyed, mad, roaring drunk.
In his arms is an earthen half-gallon jar of whisky;
streaming from one of the pockets of his coat is the arm of
a new tunic shirt; on his head is a woman's vivid blue
hat with gold lacing, all of which he has looted.*

Fluther (singing in a frenzy):

Fluther's a jolly good fella! . . . Fluther's a jolly good
    fella!
Up th' rebels! . . . That nobody can deny!

> [*He beats on the door.*

Get us a mug or a jug, or somethin', some o' yous, one o'
yous, will yous, before I lay one o' yous out! . . . (*Looking
down the street*) Bang an' fire away for all Fluther cares. . . .
(*Banging at door*) Come down an' open th' door, some of yous,
one of yous, will yous, before I lay some o' yous out! . . .
Th' whole city can topple home to hell, for Fluther!

> [*Inside the house is heard a scream from* Nora, *followed by a
> moan.*

Fluther (singing furiously):

That nobody can deny, that nobody can deny,
For Fluther's a jolly good fella, Fluther's a jolly good fella,
Fluther's a jolly good fella . . . Up th' rebels! That
    nobody can deny!

> [*His frantic movements cause him to spill some of the whisky
> out of the jar.*

Blast you, Fluther, don't be spillin' th' precious liquor!
(*He kicks at the door*).   Ay, give us a mug or a jug, or somethin',
one o' yous, some o' yous, will yous, before I lay one o' yous
out!

> [*The door suddenly opens, and* Bessie, *coming out, grips him
> by the collar.*

Bessie (indignantly).   You bowsey, come in ower o' that.

. . . I'll thrim your thricks o' dhrunken dancin' for you, an' none of us knowin' how soon we'll bump into a world we were never in before!

Fluther (as she is pulling him in). Ay, th' jar, th' jar, th' jar!

> [*A short pause, then again is heard a scream of pain from* Nora. *The door opens and Mrs.* Gogan *and* Bessie *are seen standing at it.*

Bessie. Fluther would go, only he's too dhrunk. . . . Oh, God, isn't it a pity he's so dhrunk! We'll have to thry to get a docthor somewhere.

Mrs. Gogan. I'd be afraid to go. . . . Besides, Mollser's terrible bad. I don't think you'll get a docthor to come. It's hardly any use goin'.

Bessie (determinedly). I'll risk it. . . . Give her a little of Fluther's whisky. . . . It's th' fright that's brought it on her so soon. . . . Go on back to her, you.

> [Mrs. Gogan *goes in, and* Bessie *softly closes the door. She is moving forward, when the sound of some rifle shots, and the tok, tok, tok of a distant machine-gun brings her to a sudden halt. She hesitates for a moment, then she tightens her shawl round her, as if it were a shield, then she firmly and swiftly goes out.*

Bessie (as she goes out). Oh, God, be Thou my help in time o' throuble. An' shelter me safely in th' shadow of Thy wings!

CURTAIN

ACT IV

The living-room of Bessie Burgess. ' It is one of two small attic rooms (the other, used as a bedroom, is to the Left), the ceiling slopes up towards the back, giving to the apartment a look of compressed confinement. In the centre of the ceiling is a small skylight. There is an unmistakable air of poverty bordering on destitution. The paper on the walls is torn and soiled, particularly near the fire where the cooking is done, and near the washstand where the washing is done. The fireplace is to the Left. A small armchair near fire. One small window at Back. A pane of this window is starred by the entrance of a bullet. Under the window to the Right is an oak coffin standing on two kitchen chairs. Near the coffin is a home-manufactured stool, on which are two lighted candles. Beside the window is a worn-out dresser on which is a small quantity of delf. Tattered remains of cheap lace curtains drape the window. Standing near the window on Left is a brass standard-lamp with a fancy shade; hanging on the wall near the same window is a vividly crimson silk dress, both of which have been looted. A door on Left leading to the bedroom. Another opposite giving a way to the rest of the house. To the Left of this door a common washstand. A tin kettle, very black, and an old saucepan inside the fender. There is no light in the room but that given from the two candles and the fire. The dusk has well fallen, and the glare of the burning buildings in the town can be seen through the window, in the distant sky. The Covey and Fluther have been playing cards, sitting on the floor by the light of the candles on the stool near the coffin. When the curtain rises the Covey is shuffling the cards, Peter is sitting in a stiff, dignified way beside him, and Fluther is kneeling beside the window, cautiously looking out. It is a few days later.

Fluther (*furtively peeping out of the window*). Give them a good shuffling. . . . Th' sky's gettin' reddher an' reddher. . . . You'd think it was afire. . . . Half o' th' city must be burnin'.

The Covey. If I was you, Fluther, I'd keep away from that window. . . . It's dangerous, an', besides, if they see you, you'll only bring a nose on th' house.

Peter. Yes; an' he knows we had to leave our own place th' way they were riddlin' it with machine-gun fire. . . . He'll keep on pimpin' an' pimpin' there, till we have to fly out o' this place too.

Fluther (*ironically*). If they make any attack here, we'll send you out in your green an' glory uniform, shakin' your sword over your head, an' they'll fly before you as th' Danes flew before Brian Boru!

The Covey (*placing the cards on the floor, after shuffling them*). Come on, an' cut.

[*Fluther comes over, sits on floor, and cuts the cards.*
The Covey (*having dealt the cards*). Spuds up again.

[*Nora moans feebly in room on Left.*
Fluther. There, she's at it again. She's been quiet for a long time, all th' same.

The Covey. She was quiet before, sure, an' she broke out again worse than ever. . . . What was led that time?

Peter. Thray o' Hearts, Thray o' Hearts, Thray o' Hearts.

Fluther. It's damned hard lines to think of her dead-born kiddie lyin' there in th' arms o' poor little Mollser. Mollser snuffed it sudden too, afther all.

The Covey. Sure she never got any care. How could she get it, an' th' mother out day an' night lookin' for work, an' her consumptive husband leavin' her with a baby to be born before he died!

Voices in a lilting chant to the Left in a distant street. Red Cr . . . oss, Red Cr . . . oss! . . . Ambu . . . lance, Ambu . . . lance!

The Covey (*to* Fluther). Your deal, Fluther.

Fluther (*shuffling and dealing the cards*). It'll take a lot out o' Nora—if she'll ever be th' same.

The Covey. Th' docthor thinks she'll never be th' same; thinks she'll be a little touched here. (*He touches his forehead.*) She's ramblin' a lot; thinkin' she's out in th' counthry with Jack; or gettin' his dinner ready for him before he comes home; or yellin' for her kiddie. All that, though, might be th' chloroform she got. . . . I don't know what we'd have done only for oul' Bessie; up with her for th' past three nights, hand runnin'.

Fluther. I always knew there was never anything really derogatory wrong with poor oul' Bessie. (*To* Peter, *who is taking a trick*) Ay, houl' on, there, don't be so damn quick— that's my thrick.

Peter. What's your thrick? It's my thrick, man.

Fluther (*loudly*). How is it your thrick?

Peter (*answering as loudly*). Didn't I lead th' deuce!

Fluther. You must be gettin' blind, man; don't you see th' ace?

Bessie (*appearing at the door of room, Left; in a tense whisper*). D'ye want to waken her again on me, when she's just gone asleep? If she wakes will yous come an' mind her? If I hear a whisper out o' one o' yous again, I'll . . . gut yous!

The Covey (*in a whisper*). S-s-s-h. She can hear anything above a whisper.

Peter (*looking up at the ceiling*). Th' gentle an' merciful God 'll give th' pair o' yous a scawldin' an' a scarifyin' one o' these days!

[*Fluther takes a bottle of whisky from his pocket, and takes a drink.*

The Covey (*to* Fluther). Why don't you spread that out, man, an' thry to keep a sup for to-morrow?

Fluther. Spread it out? Keep a sup for to-morrow? How th' hell does a fella know there'll be any to-morrow?

If I'm goin' to be whipped away, let me be whipped away when it's empty, an' not when it's half full! (*To Bessie, who has seated herself in an armchair at the fire*) How is she, now, Bessie?

Bessie. I left her sleeping quietly. When I'm listenin' to her babblin', I think she'll never be much betther than she is. Her eyes have a hauntin' way of lookin' in instead of lookin' out, as if her mind had been lost alive in madly minglin' memories of th' past. . . . (*Sleepily*) Crushin' her thoughts . . . together . . . in a fierce . . . an' fanciful . . . (*she nods her head and starts wakefully*) idea that dead things are livin', an' livin' things are dead. . . . (*With a start*) Was that a scream I heard her give? (*Reassured*) Blessed God, I think I hear her screamin' every minute! An' it's only there with me that I'm able to keep awake.

The Covey. She'll sleep, maybe, for a long time, now. Ten there.

Fluther. Ten here. If she gets a long sleep, she might be all right. Peter's th' lone five.

The Covey. Whisht! I think I hear somebody movin' below. Whoever it is, he's comin' up.

> [*A pause. Then the door opens and* Captain Brennan *comes into the room. He has changed his uniform for a suit of civvies. His eyes droop with the heaviness of exhaustion; his face is pallid and drawn. His clothes are dusty and stained here and there with mud. He leans heavily on the back of a chair as he stands.*

Capt. Brennan. Mrs. Clitheroe; where's Mrs. Clitheroe? I was told I'd find her here.

Bessie. What d'ye want with Mrs. Clitheroe?

Capt. Brennan. I've a message, a last message for her from her husband.

Bessie. Killed! He's not killed, is he!

Capt. Brennan (*sinking stiffly and painfully on to a chair*). In th' Imperial Hotel; we fought till th' place was in flames. He was shot through th' arm, an' then through th' lung. . . . I could do nothin' for him—only watch his breath comin' an' goin' in quick, jerky gasps, an' a tiny sthream o' blood thricklin' out of his mouth, down over his lower lip. . . . I said a prayer for th' dyin', an' twined his Rosary beads around his fingers. . . . Then I had to leave him to save meself. . . . (*He shows some holes in his coat*) Look at th' way a machine-gun tore at me coat, as I belted out o' the buildin' an' darted across th' sthreet for shelter. . . . An' then, I seen The Plough an' th' Stars fallin' like a shot as th' roof crashed in, an' where I'd left poor Jack was nothin' but a leppin' spout o' flame!

Bessie (*with partly repressed vehemence*). Ay, you left him! You twined his Rosary beads round his fingers, an' then you run like a hare to get out o' danger!

Capt. Brennan. I took me chance as well as him. . . . He took it like a man. His last whisper was to 'Tell Nora to be brave; that I'm ready to meet my God, an' that I'm proud to die for Ireland.' An' when our General heard it he said that 'Commandant Clitheroe's end was a gleam of glory.' Mrs. Clitheroe's grief will be a joy when she realizes that she has had a hero for a husband.

Bessie. If you only seen her, you'd know to th' differ.

[Nora *appears at door,* Left. *She is clad only in her night-dress; her hair, uncared for some days, is hanging in disorder over her shoulders. Her pale face looks paler still because of a vivid red spot on the tip of each cheek. Her eyes are glimmering with the light of incipient insanity; her hands are nervously fiddling with her nightgown. She halts at the door for a moment, looks vacantly around the room, and then comes slowly in. The rest do not notice her till she speaks.*

Nora (*in a quiet and monotonous tone*). No . . . Not there, Jack. . . . I can feel comfortable only in our own familiar place beneath th' bramble tree. . . . We must be walking

for a long time; I feel very, very tired. . . . Have we to go
farther, or have we passed it by? (*Passing her hand across her
eyes*) Curious mist on my eyes. . . . Why don't you hold my
hand, Jack. . . . (*Excitedly*) No, no, Jack, it's not. Can't you
see it's a goldfinch. Look at th' black-satiny wings with
th' gold bars, an' th' splash of crimson on its head. . . .
(*Wearily*) Something ails me, something ails me. . . . Don't
kiss me like that; you take my breath away, Jack. . . . Why
do you frown at me? . . . You're going away, and (*frightened*)
I can't follow you. Something's keeping me from moving.
. . . (*Crying out*) Jack, Jack, Jack!

    Bessie (*who has gone over and caught* Nora's *arm*). Now, Mrs.
Clitheroe, you're a terrible woman to get up out of bed. . . .
You'll get cold if you stay here in them clothes.

    Nora. Cold? I'm feelin' very cold; it's chilly out here
in th' counthry. . . . (*Looking around frightened*) What place
is this? Where am I?

    Bessie (*coaxingly*). You're all right, Nora; you're with
friends, an' in a safe place. Don't you know your uncle an'
your cousin, an' poor oul' Fluther?

    Peter (*about to go over to* Nora). Nora, darlin', now——

    Fluther (*pulling him back*). Now, leave her to Bessie, man.
A crowd 'll only make her worse.

    Nora (*thoughtfully*). There is something I want to re-
member, an' I can't. (*With agony*) I can't, I can't, I can't!
My head, my head! (*Suddenly breaking from* Bessie, *and running
over to the men, and gripping* Fluther *by the shoulders*) Where is it?
Where's my baby? Tell me where you've put it, where've
you hidden it? My baby, my baby; I want my baby! My
head, my poor head. . . . Oh, I can't tell what is wrong with
me. (*Screaming*) Give him to me, give me my husband!

    Bessie. Blessin' o' God on us, isn't this pitiful!

    Nora (*struggling with* Bessie). I won't go away for you;
I won't. Not till you give me back my husband. (*Screaming*)
Murderers, that's what yous are; murderers, murderers!

Bessie. S-s-sh. We'll bring Mr. Clitheroe back to you, if you'll only lie down an' stop quiet. . . . (*Trying to lead her in*) Come on, now, Nora, an' I'll sing something to you.

Nora. I feel as if my life was thryin' to foice its way out of my body. . . . I can hardly breathe . . . I'm frightened, I'm frightened, I'm frightened! For God's sake, don't leave me, Bessie. Hold my hand, put your arms around me!

Fluther (*to* Brennan). Now you can see th' way she is, man.

Peter. An' what way would she be if she heard Jack had gone west?

The Covey (*to* Peter). Shut up, you, man!

Bessie (*to* Nora). We'll have to be brave, an' let patience clip away th' heaviness of th' slow-movin' hours, rememberin' that sorrow may endure for th' night, but joy cometh in th' mornin'. . . . Come on in, an' I'll sing to you, an' you'll rest quietly.

Nora (*stopping suddenly on her way to the room*). Jack an' me are goin' out somewhere this evenin'. Where I can't tell. Isn't it curious I can't remember. . . . Maura, Maura, Jack, if th' baby's a girl; any name you like, if th' baby's a boy! . . . He's there. (*Screaming*) He's there, an' they won't give him back to me!

Bessie. S-ss-s-h, darlin', s-ssh. I won't sing to you, if you're not quiet.

Nora (*nervously holding* Bessie). Hold my hand, hold my hand, an' sing to me, sing to me!

Bessie. Come in an' lie down, an' I'll sing to you.

Nora (*vehemently*). Sing to me, sing to me; sing, sing!

Bessie (*singing as she leads* Nora *into room*):

> Lead, kindly light, amid th' encircling gloom,
>   Lead Thou me on;
> Th' night is dark an' I am far from home,
>   Lead Thou me on.

Keep Thou my feet; I do not ask to see
Th' distant scene—one step enough for me.

So long that Thou hast blessed me, sure Thou still
    Wilt lead me on;

[*They go in.*

Bessie (singing in room):

O'er moor an' fen, o'er crag an' torrent, till
    Th' night is gone.
An' in th' morn those angel faces smile
That I have lov'd long since, an' lost awhile!

The Covey (to Brennan). Now that you've seen how bad she is, an' that we daren't tell her what has happened till she's bether, you'd best be slippin' back to where you come from.

Capt. Brennan. There's no chance o' slippin' back now, for th' military are everywhere: a fly couldn't get through. I'd never have got here, only I managed to change me uniform for what I'm wearin'. . . . I'll have to take me chance, an' thry to lie low here for a while.

The Covey (frightened). There's no place here to lie low. Th' Tommies 'll be hoppin' in here, any minute!

Peter (aghast). An' then we'd all be shanghaied!

The Covey. Be God, there's enough afther happenin' to us!

Fluther (warningly, as he listens). Whisht, whisht, th' whole o' yous. I think I heard th' clang of a rifle butt on th' floor of th' hall below. (*All alertness.*) Here, come on with th' cards again. I'll deal.

[*He shuffles and deals the cards to all.*

Fluther. Clubs up. (*To* Brennan) Thry to keep your hands from shakin', man. You lead, Peter. (*As* Peter *throws out a card*) Four o' Hearts led.

[*The door opens and* Corporal Stoddart *of the Wiltshires enters in full war kit; steel helmet, rifle and bayonet, and trench tool. He looks round the room. A pause and a palpable silence*

Fluther (*breaking the silence*). Two tens an' a five.

Corporal Stoddart. 'Ello. (*Indicating the coffin*) This the stiff?

The Covey. Yis.

Corporal Stoddart. Who's gowing with it? Ownly one allowed to gow with it, you know.

The Covey. I dunno.

Corporal Stoddart. You dunnow?

The Covey. I dunno.

Bessie (*coming into the room*). She's afther slippin' off to sleep again, thanks be to God. I'm hardly able to keep me own eyes open. (*To the soldier*) Oh, are yous goin' to take away poor little Mollser?

Corporal Stoddart. Ay; 'oo's agowing with 'er?

Bessie. Oh, th' poor mother, o' course. God help her, it's a terrible blow to her!

Fluther. A terrible blow? Sure, she's in her element now, woman, mixin' earth to earth, an' ashes t'ashes an' dust to dust, an' revellin' in plumes an' hearses, last days an' judgements!

Bessie (*falling into chair by the fire*). God bless us! I'm jaded!

Corporal Stoddart. Was she plugged?

The Covey. Ah, no; died o' consumption.

Corporal Stoddart. Ow, is that all? Thought she moight 'ave been plugged.

The Covey. Is that all? Isn't it enough? D'ye know, comrade, that more die o' consumption than are killed in th' wars? An' it's all because of th' system we're livin' undher?

Corporal Stoddart. Ow, I know. I'm a Sowcialist moiself, but I 'as to do my dooty.

The Covey (*ironically*). Dooty! Th' only dooty of a Socialist is th' emancipation of th' workers.

Corporal Stoddart. Ow, a man's a man, an 'e 'as to foight for 'is country, 'asn't 'e?

Fluther (aggressively). You're not fightin' for your counthry here, are you?

Peter (anxiously, to Fluther). Ay, ay, Fluther, none o' that, none o' that!

The Covey. Fight for your counthry! Did y'ever read, comrade, Jenersky's *Thesis on the Origin, Development, an' Consolidation of th' Evolutionary Idea of the Proletariat?*

Corporal Stoddart. Ow, cheese it, Paddy, cheese it!

Bessie (sleepily). How is things in th' town, Tommy?

Corporal Stoddart. Ow, I fink it's nearly hover. We've got 'em surrounded, and we're clowsing in on the bloighters. Ow, it was only a little bit of a dawg-foight.

[*The sharp ping of the sniper's rifle is heard, followed by a squeal of pain.*

Voices to the Left in a chant. Red Cr . . . oss, Red Cr . . . oss! Ambu . . . lance, Ambu . . . lance!

Corporal Stoddart (excitedly). Christ, that's another of our men 'it by that blawsted sniper! 'E's knocking abaht 'ere, somewheres. Gawd, when we get th' bloighter, we'll give 'im the cold steel, we will. We'll jab the belly aht of 'im, we will!

[*Mrs. Gogan comes in tearfully, and a little proud of the importance of being directly connected with death.*

Mrs. Gogan (to Fluther). I'll never forget what you done for me, Fluther, goin' around at th' risk of your life settlin' everything with th' undhertaker an' th' cemetery people. When all me own were afraid to put their noses out, you plunged like a good one through hummin' bullets, an' they knockin' fire out o' th' road, tinklin' through th' frightened windows, an' splashin' themselves to pieces on th' walls! An' you'll find, that Mollser, in th' happy place she's gone to, won't forget to whisper, now an' again, th' name o' Fluther.

Corporal Stoddart. Git it aht, mother, git it aht.

Bessie (from the chair). It's excusin' me you'll be, Mrs.

Gogan, for not stannin' up, seein' I'm shaky on me feet for want of a little sleep, an' not desirin' to show any disrespect to poor little Mollser.

Fluther. Sure, we all know, Bessie, that it's vice versa with you.

Mrs. Gogan (to Bessie). Indeed, it's meself that has well chronicled, Mrs. Burgess, all your gentle hurryin's to me little Mollser, when she was alive, bringin' her somethin' to dhrink, or somethin' t'eat, an' never passin' her without liftin' up her heart with a delicate word o' kindness.

Corporal Stoddart (impatiently, but kindly). Git it aht, git it aht, mother.

> [*The* Covey, Fluther, Brennan, *and* Peter *carry out the coffin, followed by* Mrs. Gogan.

Corporal Stoddart (to Bessie, *who is almost asleep).* 'Ow many men is in this 'ere 'ouse? (*No answer. Loudly*) 'Ow many men is in this 'ere 'ouse?

Bessie (waking with a start). God, I was nearly asleep ! . . . How many men? Didn't you see them?

Corporal Stoddart. Are they all that are in the 'ouse?

Bessie. Oh, there's none higher up, but there may be more lower down. Why?

Corporal Stoddart. All men in the district 'as to be rounded up. Somebody's giving 'elp to the snipers, an we 'as to take precautions. If I 'ad my woy, I'd make 'em all join hup, and do their bit ! But I suppowse they and you are all Shinners.

Bessie (who has been sinking into sleep, waking up to a sleepy vehemence). Bessie Burgess is no Shinner, an' never had no thruck with anything spotted be th' fingers o' th' Fenians; but always made it her business to harness herself for Church whenever she knew that God Save the King was goin' to be sung at t'end of th' service; whose only son went to th' front in th' first contingent of the Dublin Fusiliers, an' that's on his way home carryin' a shatthered arm that he got fightin' for his King an' counthry !

[*Her head sinks slowly forward again. Peter comes into the room; his body is stiffened and his face is wearing a comically indignant look. He walks to and fro at the back of the room, evidently repressing a violent desire to speak angrily. He is followed in by* Fluther, *the* Covey, *and* Brennan, *who slinks into an obscure corner of the room, nervous of notice.*

Fluther (after an embarrassing pause). Th' air in th' sthreet outside's shakin' with th' firin' o' rifles an' machine-guns. It must be a hot shop in th' middle o' th' scrap.

Corporal Stoddart. We're pumping lead in on 'em from every side, now; they'll soon be shoving up th' white flag.

Peter (with a shout). I'm tellin' you either o' yous two lowsers 'ud make a betther hearse-man than Peter; proddin' an' pokin' at me an' I helpin' to carry out a corpse!

Fluther. It wasn't a very derogatory thing for th' Covey to say that you'd make a fancy hearse-man, was it?

Peter (furiously). A pair o' redjesthered bowseys pondherin' from mornin' till night on how they'll get a chance to break a gap through th' quiet nature of a man that's always endeavourin' to chase out of him any sthray thought of venom against his fella-man!

The Covey. Oh, shut it, shut it, shut it!

Peter. As long as I'm a livin' man, responsible for me thoughts, words, an' deeds to th' Man above, I'll feel meself instituted to fight again' th' sliddherin' ways of a pair o' picaroons, whisperin', concurrin', concoctin', an' conspirin' together to rendher me unconscious of th' life I'm thryin' to live!

Corporal Stoddart (dumbfounded). What's wrong, Daddy; wot 'ave they done to you?

Peter (savagely to the Corporal). You mind your own business! What's it got to do with you, what's wrong with me?

Bessie (in a sleepy murmur). Will yous thry to conthrol yourselves into quietness? Yous'll waken her . . . up . . . on . . . me . . . again.   [*She sleeps.*

Fluther. Come on, boys, to th' cards again, an' never mind him.

Corporal Stoddart. No use of you gowing to start cawds; you'll be gowing out of 'ere, soon as Sergeant comes.

Fluther. Goin' out o' here? An' why're we goin' out o' here?

Corporal Stoddart. All men in district to be rounded up, and 'eld in till the scrap is hover.

Fluther. An' where're we goin' to be held in?

Corporal Stoddart. They're puttin 'em in a church.

The Covey. A church?

Fluther. What sort of a church? Is it a Protestan' Church?

Corporal Stoddart. I dunnow; I suppowse so.

Fluther (dismayed). Be God, it'll be a nice thing to be stuck all night in a Protestan' Church!

Corporal Stoddart. Bring the cawds; you moight get a chance of a goime.

Fluther. Ah, no, that wouldn't do. . . . I wondher? (*After a moment's thought*) Ah, I don't think we'd be doin' anything derogatory be playin' cards in a Protestan' Church.

Corporal Stoddart. If I was you I'd bring a little snack with me; you moight be glad of it before the mawning. (*Sings*) :

> I do loike a snoice mince poy,
> I do loike a snoice mince poy!

[*The snap of the sniper's rifle rings out again, followed simultaneously by a scream of pain. Corporal Stoddart goes pale, and brings his rifle to the ready, listening.*

Voices chanting to the Right. Red Cro . . . ss, Red Cro . . . ss! Ambu . . . lance, Ambu . . . lance!

[*Sergeant Tinley comes rapidly in, pale, agitated, and fiercely angry.*

Corporal Stoddart (to Sergeant). One of hour men 'it, Sergeant?

Sergeant Tinley. Private Taylor; got 'it roight through the chest, 'e did; an 'ole in front of 'im as 'ow you could put your fist through, and 'arf 'is back blown awoy! Dum-dum bullets they're using. Gang of Hassassins potting at us from behind roofs. That's not playing the goime: why down't they come into the owpen and foight fair!

Fluther (unable to stand the slight). Fight fair! A few hundhred scrawls o' chaps with a couple o' guns an' Rosary beads, again' a hundhred thousand thrained men with horse, fut, an' artillery . . . an' he wants us to fight fair! (*To* Sergeant) D'ye want us to come out in our skins an' throw stones?

Sergeant Tinley (to Corporal). Are these four all that are 'ere?

Corporal Stoddart. Four; that's all, Sergeant.

Sergeant Tinley (vindictively). Come on, then; get the blighters aht. (*To the men*) 'Ere, 'op it aht! Aht into the streets with you, and if a snoiper sends another of our men west, you gow with 'im! (*He catches Fluther by the shoulder*) Gow on, git aht!

Fluther. Eh, who are you chuckin', eh?

Sergeant Tinley (roughly). Gow on, git aht, you blighter.

Fluther. Who are you callin' a blighter to, eh? I'm a Dublin man, born an' bred in th' city, see?

Sergeant Tinley. I down't care if you were Broin Buroo; git aht, git aht.

Fluther (halting as he is going out). Jasus, you an' your guns! Leave them down, an' I'd beat th' two o' yous without sweatin'!

> [Peter, Brennan, *the* Covey, *and* Fluther, *followed by the soldiers, go out. Bessie is sleeping heavily on the chair by the fire. After a pause,* Nora *appears at door, Left, in her nightdress. Remaining at door for a few moments she looks vaguely around the room. She then comes in quietly, goes over to the fire, pokes it, and puts the kettle*

*on. She thinks for a few moments, pressing her hand to
her forehead. She looks questioningly at the fire, and then
at the press at back. She goes to the press, opens it, takes
out a soiled cloth and spreads it on the table. She then
places things for tea on the table.*

Nora. I imagine th' room looks very odd somehow. . . .
I was nearly forgetting Jack's tea. . . . Ah, I think I'll have
everything done before he gets in. . . . (*She lilts gently, as she
arranges the table.*)

> Th' violets were scenting th' woods, Nora,
>   Displaying their charms to th' bee,
> When I first said I lov'd only you, Nora,
>   An' you said you lov'd only me.
>
> Th' chestnut blooms gleam'd through th' glade,
>   Nora,
>   A robin sang loud from a tree,
> When I first said I lov'd only you, Nora,
>   An' you said you lov'd only me.

                    [*She pauses suddenly, and glances round the room.*
Nora (*doubtfully*). I can't help feelin' this room very
strange. . . . What is it? . . . What is it? . . . I must
think. . . . I must thry to remember. . . .

Voices chanting in a distant street. Ambu . . . lance, Ambu
. . . lance! Red Cro . . . ss, Red Cro . . . ss!

Nora (*startled and listening for a moment, then resuming the
arrangement of the table*):

> Trees, birds, an' bees sang a song, Nora,
>   Of happier transports to be,
> When I first said I lov'd only you, Nora,
>   An' you said you lov'd only me.

    [*A burst of rifle fire is heard in a street near by, followed
    by the rapid rok, tok, tok of a machine-gun.*

Nora (*staring in front of her and screaming*).   Jack, Jack, Jack!
My baby, my baby, my baby!

Bessie (*waking with a start*).   You divil, are you afther gettin'
out o' bed again!

> [*She rises and runs towards* Nora, *who rushes to the window,
> which she frantically opens.*

Nora (*at window, screaming*).   Jack, Jack, for God's sake,
come to me!

Soldiers (*outside, shouting*).   Git away, git away from that
window, there!

Bessie (*seizing hold of* Nora).   Come away, come away,
woman, from that window!

Nora (*struggling with* Bessie).   Where is it; where have you
hidden it?   Oh, Jack, Jack, where are you?

Bessie (*imploringly*).   Mrs. Clitheroe, for God's sake, come
away!

Nora (*fiercely*).   I won't; he's below. Let . . . me . . .
go!   You're thryin' to keep me from me husband.   I'll
follow him.   Jack, Jack, come to your Nora!

Bessie.   Hus-s-sh, Nora, Nora!   He'll be here in a minute.
I'll bring him to you, if you'll only be quiet—honest to God, I will.

> [*With a great effort* Bessie *pushes* Nora *away from the
> window, the force used causing her to stagger against it
> herself.   Two rifle shots ring out in quick succession.
> Bessie jerks her body convulsively; stands stiffly for a
> moment, a look of agonized astonishment on her face,
> then she staggers forward, leaning heavily on the table
> with her hands.*

Bessie (*with an arrested scream of fear and pain*).   Merciful
God, I'm shot, I'm shot, I'm shot! . . . Th' life's pourin' out
o' me!   (*To* Nora)   I've got this through . . . through
you . . . through you, you bitch, you! . . . O God, have
mercy on me! . . . (*To* Nora)   You wouldn't stop quiet, no,
you wouldn't, you wouldn't, blast you!   Look at what I'm
afther gettin', look at what I'm afther gettin' . . . I'm

bleedin' to death, an' no one's here to stop th' flowin' blood!
(*Calling*) Mrs. Gogan, Mrs. Gogan! Fluther, Fluther, for
God's sake, somebody, a doctor, a doctor!

> [*She staggers frightened towards the door, to seek for aid,
> but, weakening half-way across the room, she sinks to her
> knees, and bending forward, supports herself with her
> hands resting on the floor. Nora is standing rigidly with
> her back to the wall opposite, her trembling hands held out
> a little from the sides of her body, her lips quivering, her
> breast heaving, staring wildly at the figure of Bessie.*

Nora (*in a breathless whisper*). Jack, I'm frightened. . . .
I'm frightened, Jack. . . . Oh, Jack, where are you?

Bessie (*moaning*). This is what's afther comin' on me for
nursin' you day an' night. . . . I was a fool, a fool, a fool!
Get me a dhrink o' wather, you jade, will you? There's a
fire burnin' in me blood! (*Pleadingly*) Nora, Nora, dear, for
God's sake, run out an' get Mrs. Gogan, or Fluther, or somebody to bring a doctor, quick, quick, quick! (*As Nora does
not stir*) Blast you, stir yourself, before I'm gone!

Nora. Oh, Jack, Jack, where are you?

Bessie (*in a whispered moan*). Jesus Christ, me sight's goin'!
It's all dark, dark! Nora, hold me hand!

> [*Bessie's body lists over and she sinks into a prostrate position
> on the floor.*

Bessie. I'm dyin', I'm dyin' . . . I feel it. . . . Oh
God, oh God! (*She feebly sings*)

> I do believe, I will believe
>   That Jesus died for me;
> That on th' cross He shed His blood,
>   From sin to set me free. . . .
>
> I do believe . . . I will believe
>   . . . Jesus died . . . me;
> . . . th' cross He shed . . . blood,
>   From sin . . . free.

[*She ceases singing, and lies stretched out, still and very rigid.
A pause. Then* Mrs. Gogan *runs hastily in.*

Mrs. Gogan (*quivering with fright*). Blessed be God, what's
afther happenin'? (*To* Nora) What's wrong, child, what's
wrong? (*She sees* Bessie, *runs to her and bends over the body*) Bessie,
Bessie! (*She shakes the body*) Mrs. Burgess, Mrs. Burgess!
(*She feels* Bessie's *forehead*) My God, she's as cold as death.
They're afther murdherin' th' poor inoffensive woman!

[*Sergeant Tinley and* Corporal Stoddart *enter agitatedly,
their rifles at the ready.*

Sergeant Tinley (*excitedly*). This is the 'ouse. That's the window!

Nora (*pressing back against the wall*). Hide it, hide it; cover
it up, cover it up!

Sergeant Tinley (*going over to the body*). 'Ere, what's this?
Who's this? (*Looking at* Bessie) Oh Gawd, we've plugged one
of the women of the 'ouse.

Corporal Stoddart. Whoy the 'ell did she gow to the window?
Is she dead?

Sergeant Tinley. Oh, dead as bedamned. Well, we
couldn't afford to toike any chawnces.

Nora (*screaming*). Hide it, hide it; don't let me see it!
Take me away, take me away, Mrs. Gogan!

[Mrs. Gogan *runs into room,* Left, *and runs out again with
a sheet which she spreads over the body of* Bessie.

Mrs. Gogan (*as she spreads the sheet*). Oh, God help her, th'
poor woman, she's stiffenin' out as hard as she can! Her face
has written on it th' shock o' sudden agony, an' her hands is
whitenin' into th' smooth shininess of wax.

Nora (*whimperingly*). Take me away, take me away;
don't leave me here to be lookin' an' lookin' at it!

Mrs. Gogan (*going over to* Nora *and putting her arm around
her*). Come on with me, dear, an' you can doss in poor
Mollser's bed, till we gather some neighbours to come an'
give th' last friendly touches to Bessie in th' lonely layin' of
her out.   [Mrs. Gogan *and* Nora *go slowly out.*

Corporal Stoddart (*who has been looking around, to* Sergeant Tinley). Tea here, Sergeant. Wot abaht a cup of scald?

Sergeant Tinley Pour it aht, Stoddart, pour it aht. I could scoff hanything just now.

> [*Corporal Stoddart pours out two cups of tea, and the two soldiers begin to drink. In the distance is heard a bitter burst of rifle and machine-gun fire, interspersed with the boom, boom of artillery. The glare in the sky seen through the window flares into a fuller and a deeper red.*

Sergeant Tinley. There gows the general attack on the Powst Office.

Voices in a distant street. Ambu . . . lance, Ambu . . . lance! Red Cro . . . ss, Red Cro . . . ss!

> [*The voices of soldiers at a barricade outside the house are heard singing:*

> They were summoned from the 'illside,
> They were called in from the glen,
> And the country found 'em ready
> At the stirring call for men.
> Let not tears add to their 'ardship,
> As the soldiers pass along,
> And although our 'eart is breaking,
> Make it sing this cheery song.

Sergeant Tilney and Corporal Stoddart (*joining in the chorus, as they sip the tea*):

> Keep the 'owme fires burning,
> While your 'earts are yearning;
> Though your lads are far away
> They dream of 'owme;
> There's a silver loining
> Through the dark cloud shoining,
> Turn the dark cloud inside out,
> Till the boys come 'owme!

CURTAIN